★ ★ ★

PRAISE FOR

JOHN SIMMONS & *HOW TO BE LIKE PAT WILLIAMS*

"Pat Williams is the godfather of front office executives. Over the years, he has taught me about staying positive during the ebbs and flows of life. I even have a saved voicemail he left me that I listen to when I need some encouragement. Pat is a special guy who anyone would benefit from hearing speak. This book has captured how making a way for others should be a priority for anyone trying to improve in sports, business, or life."

Howie Roseman
EVP/General Manager, Philadelphia Eagles

"In my mind, Pat Williams is one of the best leaders in the history of professional sports. He has enjoyed tremendous success in his career but remains extremely humble. We can all learn from his amazing career, and we will all be better if we are more like Pat. This book is a must read for anyone interested in a career in professional sports, or anyone interested in true, servant leadership."

Mark Murphy
President and CEO, Green Bay Packers

"Only occasionally in a lifetime do you meet a truly unique person and personality. I didn't know that when I first met Pat Williams back when I was a fledgling author, and he was the youngest general manager in pro sports.

But I was privileged to help Pat write his very first book, *The Gingerbread Man*. Now, more than 90 titles from him later, I understand what a privilege it was to work with him and become his friend. You couldn't do much better than to be like Pat."

Jerry B. Jenkins
Author, *The Left Behind* series and *The Chosen* novels

"Pat Williams is one of those people you meet and go, 'Wow, how does he do all of what he does?' For John Simmons to put into words Pat's game plan for this earth life is awesome. We can use this information in our day to day lives. *How to Be Like Pat Williams: The Amazing Life of a Waymaker* maps it out for us why spirituality is important; why having a good daily attitude is important; why family is important, and the list goes on.

I've read most of Pat's books and have talked to Pat often over the years. When I'm finished with one of his books, phone calls, or in person visits I feel uplifted. No negatives, just a vision of moving through life with positive energy. Congratulations to Pat and John on helping to make all of us better people!"

Andy Reid
Head Coach, Kansas City Chiefs; Superbowl Champion

"Pat Williams has been a friend of mine for more than 20 years and is one of the most dynamic people I've had the pleasure to know—maybe the most dynamic. If you want to understand what it takes to live a full and rewarding life, read this book."

Mike Sielski
Author, *The Rise: Kobe Bryant* and *The Pursuit of Immortality*; Co-author, *How to Be Like Jackie Robinson: Life Lessons from Baseball's Greatest Hero*

"I have known Pat for over 60 years going all the way back to our days at Indiana University when I was a player, and he was a color analyst for our games on radio. He was so good that most of the people on campus watched television games but turned the sound down to listen to him and his partner do the games on radio. I knew then and I know now that Pat is one of the finest people I've ever known. He is intelligent, witty, humorous, informed, and God's man. He has been successful wherever he has gone, from the baseball fields in the minor leagues to the NBA court in Philadelphia, Chicago, and Orlando. He was ahead of his time in the marketing and promotional arena for these different pro team franchises. He is a man that lives by God's word in every aspect of his life, from the many children he has raised to the business arena, and throughout his personal life. Pat is someone I have revered and valued all these years and will continue to do so until the Lord calls us home."

Jon McGlocklin

NBA Player; Announcer, Milwaukee Bucks

"I would like to give Pat a pat on the back for this book. In it, one will clearly learn the attractive qualities of being a Waymaker versus being a Trailblazer. Waymakers help make a way for others, whereas Trailblazers blaze the trail which makes it more difficult for others to follow."

Pastor/Coach Aeneas Williams

NFL Pro Football Hall Of Famer

HOW TO BE LIKE

★ ★ PAT ★ ★

WILLIAMS

JOHN SIMMONS

HOW TO BE LIKE
PAT
WILLIAMS

THE AMAZING LIFE OF A WAYMAKER

Advantage | Books

Published by Advantage, Charleston, South Carolina.
Member of Advantage Media.

ADVANTAGE is a registered trademark, and the Advantage colophon is a trademark of Advantage Media Group, Inc.

Printed in the United States of America.

10 9 8 7 6 5 4 3 2 1

ISBN: 978-1-64225-825-7 (Paperback)
ISBN: 978-1-64225-824-0 (eBook)

LCCN: 2023903102

Cover design by Megan Elger.
Layout design by David Taylor.

This publication is designed to provide accurate and authoritative information in regard to the subject matter covered. It is sold with the understanding that the publisher is not engaged in rendering legal, accounting, or other professional services. If legal advice or other expert assistance is required, the services of a competent professional person should be sought.

Advantage Media helps busy entrepreneurs, CEOs, and leaders write and publish a book to grow their business and become the authority in their field. Advantage authors comprise an exclusive community of industry professionals, idea-makers, and thought leaders. Do you have a book idea or manuscript for consideration? We would love to hear from you at **AdvantageMedia.com**.

For Momma, my first waymaker

CONTENTS

FOREWORD

Pat Williams is a difference maker. A risk taker. A loyal friend. A fierce encourager. And a true blessing to everyone fortunate enough to meet him. He sees the good in those around him, and he's not afraid to tell you all about the potential *you* have for greatness. A conversation with him fires you up and leaves you ready to take on the world. If it sounds like I'm being overcomplimentary of this man, I promise you I'm not. I can say all this with 100 percent certainty because I have had the gift of knowing him since the moment I came into this world. Friends, I'm so excited for you to walk through these pages and get to know this amazing man whom I get to call Dad.

Growing up, I always wondered how my dad was so excited to leave for work in the morning and why he was always in a good mood when he came home. I now understand: it was because he was (and still is) extremely passionate about living every day to the fullest. And through his example, he has inspired so many others to do the same. He is never without an encouraging word, a motivating quip, and an eye out for how he can help those around him live out their full potential too.

As much as I admire my dad, I'll be honest: I wasn't too sure about the title of this book at first. You see, I'm a Christian music artist, and there's a big worship song with the same title. Of course, I'm thinking of Michael W. Smith's popular piece referencing the *ultimate* Waymaker. He is and always will be the One whom my dad and I look to when we hear that term. But as I began to think about all the doors Dad has opened and opportunities he has so willingly created for others, I began to realize that the Lord really has used my dad in a mighty way here on this earth. Everything my dad has done during his life has been with the deep God-given desire to point people to the One who's made a way for all of us to spend eternity with Him.

I believe the biggest compliment is when someone who knows you best and has "seen behind the curtain" in your life can still call you the greatest person they've ever known. Well, friends, that's how I feel about Pat Williams. As his daughter, I've seen him at his highest, his lowest, and everywhere in between—and I can tell you that he is someone we can all learn from.

So I hope after reading this book, you'll believe the potential *you* have to be the same type of person, leader, believer, world changer, and waymaker as my dad. I hope his nonstop energy and zeal for life jump off the pages through these stories John Simmons has put together and inspire you to believe you were made for more. I hope that through my dad's life, you will begin to see how the Lord weaves people into our path at just the right moments—to remind us we are not alone on the road that lies ahead. No matter how bright—or how dark—that road may sometimes seem, the ultimate Waymaker has us safe in the palm of His hand. That's the story my dad's life has to tell. Enjoy it and be inspired!

Karyn Williams
(January 2021, Nashville)

★ ★ ★

PREFACE

Disney. Lincoln. King. These are the names that drew me toward a book on the bottom shelf at a LifeWay Christian store I worked at in 2015. They were iconic names of culture and influence. All of whom portrayed a specific characteristic of leadership such as vision, a serving heart, and communication. Little did I know that the person who would become the most influential example to my own life was also listed on the cover—but not as one of the leaders. He was the author.

21 Great Leaders, by Pat Williams, was the first book I read as an adult that caused me to take literal notes. I pulled out scrap paper and began writing when I noticed similarities between the leaders. I first saw that many leaders began their greatest works or periods of influence in their thirties. I also noted that many of the leaders dealt with some serious setbacks and failures during their journey. My notes began to swell from all the lessons I wrote down.

The stories I read in *21 Great Leaders* were inspiring, encouraging, and motivating. Yet they were not what captured my greatest curiosity from the book. Instead, I was intrigued most by a sentence on the back cover. Pat Williams is a motivational speaker, author of ninety books, and senior vice president of the National Basketball Association (NBA) team the Orlando Magic.

My first thought when reading that sentence was "How does anyone have the time to write ninety books?" I quickly followed that thought with "Since this book has taught me so much, what other books could I get by Pat?" A quick Google search for Pat Williams's books led me to a tremendous discovery—an even greater list of his accomplishments.

In addition to his writing more than a hundred books, I quickly learned that Pat had also run fifty-eight marathons, beaten cancer, climbed Mount Rainier, hosted a radio show, taught a Sunday school class, and, of course, was a founder and executive for the Orlando Magic. I had never heard of him before I'd first picked up *21 Great Leaders*, but his story sounded as fascinating as any of the testimonies of the great leaders I had just read about.

On the last page of the book, it said, "We would love to hear from you. Please send your comments about this book to Pat Williams at the above address." I had never seen such a request from an author in any other book I had read. I had also never gotten so much out of a book. I wanted to let Pat know how much I'd learned but stalled as I contemplated if writing a letter to Pat would be worth the time. I thought, "My letter would be buried in a mountain of other letters" and "He would never see it."

The notes I had taken stared back at me. I had just gotten so much out of this book. I thought, "If someone read my work and got that much out of it, I would love to know." So I mailed a handwritten letter to Pat Williams describing many of the lessons I'd learned from his book *21 Great Leaders*. I also shared a little bit about myself and my work in ministry. I had no expectations for what was to come. I only wanted Pat to know I'd learned something from him.

Several weeks later, I opened a hardly used side door to my home. A bright blue package that had been inside the screen door fell at my feet. The words *Orlando Magic* looked up at me. I was confused and thought, "I haven't ordered anything." Inside I found another handwritten note, but this time it was from Pat Williams. He thanked me for taking the time to write and send him a letter. He also sent me a copy of his newest book and a business card with his contact information. These contents were unexpected but warmly received. I was thankful for his time and consideration.

When I read *21 Great Leaders*, I wasn't expecting that the most impactful lessons I would learn would come from looking at the life of the author instead of the subjects of his writing. I never thought a man as busy as Pat would take the time to respond to my letter. I also couldn't have imagined that the letter would launch a longer voyage of waymaking lessons and conversations with this great man of God.

In the time since, I have had the privilege of speaking with Pat on my radio and live streaming programs. In addition, Pat was gracious enough to write the foreword for my previous book, *God Has a Sentence for Your Life*. Those brief moments of conversation and personal attention have meant the world to me. My time with Pat led me to learn my story is not unique. Pat has a habit of responding to every letter, call, and request he receives with advice, opportunities, or encouragement. In fact, he does that with almost everyone he meets. So I set out on a journey to uncover some of those stories.

The stories contained in this book are the observations and lessons learned from hundreds of people who have encountered the kindness, encouragement, and love of Pat Williams. I may not have expected much from Pat at first, but to know Pat is to learn there is much you can expect. He is a wise man of integrity, consideration, and intention. I am honored to share this collection with you. ★

INTRODUCTION

WHO DO YOU WANT TO BE LIKE WHEN YOU GROW UP?

Can you recall the days of your youth? A time when you dreamed of being like someone else? You may have said something like "I want to be like Martin Luther King Jr., Steve Jobs, or Jane Austen." You may have seen yourself on stage, performing like Justin Bieber or Carrie Underwood. You may have considered breaking new ground in science or invention like Albert Einstein and Thomas Edison.

For those who grew up playing sports, you may have wanted to be the next Babe Ruth, Serena Williams, or Hulk Hogan. If you were anything like me, you may have even pretended to be your sports heroes. In the mid-'90s, you could have found me pretending to be Michael Jordan in my Chicago Bulls jersey at the basketball court behind my childhood home. I would count down the seconds before turning around to shoot a buzzer-beater to win an imaginary championship.

In addition to all the prominent names and positions we have just mentioned, there are some people whose lives are similarly impactful—but without the fanfare. There are people who live their lives lifting up the names of the celebrated. These types of people are not usually known on a national stage but are held in high regard in certain circles. These types of people are what I call waymakers. Their lives are lived in a way that creates connection, opportunities, and fortune for others as much as for themselves.

Waymakers can achieve fame or become financially wealthy, but more often their true wealth should be measured from the perspective of the people's lives they have touched. Waymakers are people who have the potential to create ripples in the world around them. Those ripples turn to waves in the lives of others, lifting them to a place where they can sail to amazing shores.

Similar to a trailblazer, a waymaker is a pioneer. While they both create paths for others to follow, there is a difference. A trailblazer will often linger at the terminus of their mountain path of success, while a waymaker will find the energy to go back where he or she started and find others to lead. That doesn't make trailblazers bad leaders. Quite the opposite. Trailblazing is hard and often inspiring work, so it can be hard to find the energy to come back to the beginning of a path in order to lead others to the top—especially if that path took a long time to create.

The extra effort given to return to the start of a path in order to lead others is what differentiates a trailblazer from a waymaker. Another way to say it would be that all waymakers are trailblazers, but not all trailblazers are waymakers. A waymaker sees their life as a tool to guide, encourage, and love others. The pioneering actions a waymaker takes are motivated by the desire to help others. The successes of a waymaker are not for their own benefit. Instead, their lives create learnable lessons for those they guide later on.

This book is about such a person—Pat Williams, a visionary, an innovator, and a connector. The successes of Pat's life are many. His innovative ideas and promotions have become common practices in professional sports. He has brought new teams into existence. He has orchestrated a championship season. Pat is also the architect behind many well-known sports stories of the past fifty years. Pat has consistently come back down the mountain to show others the paths that they can take to find success in their own lives.

When I combined my Pat experiences with those of so many who've know him, I have found that his testimony could be lifted to a place of rarefied air. I could easily equate the humble God-fearing life Pat has lived with many well-known names of my Christian faith. I could also see his success and love for serving others lift him to equal heights of icons in secular business and leadership. Pat has a foot in both worlds but is uniquely held in high esteem in each, which is a feat not easily done.

As you will learn, Pat has been able to accomplish incredible things while also helping others achieve greatness in their lives, as well. He learned that his life was not his own. In the gospel of Luke, Jesus says the greatest two commandments are to "Love the Lord your God with all your heart, all your soul, all your strength, and all your mind. And love your neighbor as yourself."

Pat has exemplified the above lesson from Jesus in his life by living in service to both God and man. So for anyone thinking "Why would I want to be like Pat?" the answer is that Pat tries to exemplify the life Jesus taught us to live. While not perfect, his life can give both you and me hope that we can find successes in our lives by also trying to live a life like Jesus did—which is to focus on loving God and others above ourselves.

My hope with this book is not to tell the incredible journey of Pat Williams's life or to simply share the lessons his life has taught me and so many others. (Even though we will do some of both!) My hope for this book is to encourage every person who has dreamed of being someone famous or exemplary to reconsider his or her choice. I want to try to give a new kind of answer to the question "Who do you want to be like when you grow up?" There isn't a right or wrong answer to this question. I am only interested in exploring the idea that there is a certain type of person we could all strive to be like when we grow up—a waymaker. ★

WAYMAKING 101

★ ★ ★

CHAPTER ONE

BECOME A PATHFINDER

The title of this chapter, as are the other chapters of this book, is a directive for how to be like Pat Williams. When followed, the instructions of each chapter title can also help you become a waymaker. In this book, our chapter lessons will be split into two sections. The first section will be "Waymaking 101." The second section will consist of advanced studies.

In "Waymaking 101," our early chapters will cover the foundational lessons of becoming a waymaker—which are those broad ideals, traits, and decisions that Pat has made or exhibited to get where he is today. These foundational lessons will likely be commonplace among the lives of anyone who lives as a waymaker. They should also give anyone interested in becoming a waymaker a road map for how to travel.

Section two transitions the reader into advanced waymaking. These chapters represent unique, situational, and specific examples of Pat's life. The lessons and stories shared in those chapters may be uncommon among waymakers. Instead, they highlight intentional choices Pat made that lifted his ability to lead and guide others into a higher level of waymaking. Think of section one as a map to get to Waymaker Island and section two as the map to finding some of the island's treasures.

Our first lesson in "Waymaking 101" is to become a pathfinder. Before a waymaker can create a path for someone else to follow, they must first find their own path to take. For those of you without much information as to who Pat Williams is or the career he has had, this chapter will tell the story of his early days in school through the end of his baseball career as a player. For those of us who know Pat or are trying to glean from his life lessons, this section will cover the choices and opportunities Pat faced in those years. Either way, we are now embarking on a path to learn about how to live like a waymaker.

> **For anyone looking to find their own path to take in life, it's worth noting that Pat had his eyes on what he wanted to do in life early on. He lives to chase visions in his life.**

For anyone looking to find their own path to take in life, it's worth noting that Pat had his eyes on what he wanted to do in life early on. How he lives today is no different. He lives to chase visions in his life. As you will see throughout this book, if he found something that attracted his attention, even if it was something other than his main life plans, he would spend time walking down that road to see if that activity or opportunity would also become a new path his life should take. He was then able to determine which paths were worth traveling and which needed to be abandoned.

Waymakers create paths for themselves and for others. They are able to do that mainly by chasing specific visions for their lives. They are also able to discover what does or does not belong in their lives through experiences along the way. Waymakers don't often travel one path; they know many paths. They are pathfinders. I therefore find it no coincidence that the first three letters in *path* spell *Pat*.

Pat's First Paths

Patrick Livingston Murphy Williams was born in Philadelphia, Pennsylvania, in 1940, but Pat's parents, James and Ellen, raised him and his two sisters in Wilmington, Delaware. Pat's youngest sister, Mary Ellen, was born with special needs and lived in an assisted-living facility. From an early age, sports became a big part of Pat's life. James was a baseball coach, and Pat watched his dad's games and practices from the bench as a young boy. Pat's mom also took great interest in the game.

From an early age, Pat Williams knew he wanted to get into professional sports. His initial desire was to play major league baseball, and the first vision of a path for his life was sparked the moment his dad took him to his first major league game. "June 15, 1947. I remember it like it was yesterday," Pat said. "The Philadelphia A's. Connie Mack was still managing. Lou Boudreau was managing the Cleveland Indians. And there I was, immediately stricken by the sounds, the sights, and the atmosphere of baseball. I remember the color. Everything was green, the green grass and green seats and green fences; it left a huge imprint on me."

Pat woke up the next morning with his future mapped out in his mind. "I knew exactly what I wanted to do with my life. I wanted to be a ball player." Over the years, Pat has realized how important chasing that vision was to his life. He said, "Not every seven-year-old knows what they want to do with their life. I've run into many in their twenties and thirties who were still trying to figure out what they want to do in their life or what their purpose is. But at that young age, I knew exactly what I was planted on this earth for, and I did everything in my power to achieve that goal of being a ball player through my early years."

In the 1940s, youth baseball leagues were rare if not nonexistent. Pat's children and grandchildren, many of whom spent much of their childhood in the warm state of Florida, were able to play and practice baseball and other sports more than he was. "I have ten-year-old grandchildren who have played more baseball games today than I did through the end of high school," Pat said about the difference between opportunities to practice his pursuit of playing baseball professionally. "It's just amazing the opportunity youngsters have today in all endeavors, which we didn't have back in the '40s and '50s."

Almost every Saturday as a youth was spent going to Shibe Park in Philadelphia—which at the time was home to two Major League Baseball (MLB) teams. Pat and his family would make the hour-long drive to the park to watch the Phillies and the Athletics play alternating home games. Pat often arrived early enough to watch batting practice or go near the clubhouse. Pat's childhood friend Gil Yule would often go to games with him, and said, "We were into autograph collecting at Shibe Park. We would go get signatures from various A's and Phillies players."

Rick Porter went to Tower Hill School and played baseball with Pat. He remembers noticing how Pat's fascination with baseball was greater than some of the other guys on the team. He said, "I spent a lot of nights [over at Pat's house]. He had more sport magazine pages up on his bedroom walls than anybody I ever saw."

In addition to his love for baseball, Gil was also a big ice hockey fan and said that Pat sent him "clippings of the Detroit Red Wings and Chicago Blackhawks games, even though he didn't follow hockey at all." This is noteworthy because Gil may have been the first person to receive newspaper clippings from Pat—which has since become a staple activity. Friends and family will often get envelopes full of articles and stories from Pat that relate to that person's particular interests or hobbies.

For most of those trips to Shibe Park, it was Pat's mom, Ellen, who accompanied him and encouraged his curiosity in the sport. She would bring a book or a newspaper to read so Pat could involve

Pat's father's love for American history and baseball rubbed off on him in a big way.

himself with pregame baseball activities around the park. "In a way, she put my parenting to shame," Pat said about his mom in our conversation about his early life. "I've never said to one of my children 'We're going to take a drive for an hour every weekend because I know you love this activity, and I'm going to sit there with you two hours before it starts. And then I'm going to bring you home.'"

He paused and let out a sigh. The weight of that realization seemed to stir up strong feelings of love and possibly some remorse in his heart. "And you know, her whole day was devoted to that. And to do that for me for a whole baseball season for seven years. That's a huge sacrifice for a parent."

Pat's father, James, was a history teacher at Tower Hill School—a private college prep school in Wilmington from which Pat graduated in June 1958. Pat's dad had left the school by the time Pat would have been one of his students, but his father's love for American history and baseball rubbed off on him in a big way. In addition, Pat saw waymaker tendencies in his father surrounding the life of his youngest sibling—whom the family called Mimi. "Mary Ellen was born in 1947. She had a tremendous impact on our family and eventually the state of Delaware," Pat said about his sister. "My mom and dad took such an interest in helping and spearheading efforts to raise money to help these different organizations that were dealing with these children. The biggest one was the Delaware All-Star High School Football Game."

The exhibition game was a benefit event founded by Pat's dad, James Williams, and his dad's friend Bob Carpenter—who was then the owner of the Philadelphia Phillies, as well as the father of Pat's childhood best friend, Ruly. Since 1956, the Blue-Gold All-Star Game, as it was called, has been held annually in August. Former Delaware governor and Pat's Tower Hill classmate Mike Castle knows firsthand the impact of the event, and said, "It's been a big success. It's done well. They bring in cheerleaders. They bring in some of the children who have disabilities. It's an upbeat thing, and I think the people who played in it are rather proud of that fact."

"It has raised millions of dollars over the years for help and assistance to that world of Down syndrome children," Pat added about the Blue-Gold game, before reflecting on the impact his sister and his parents' handling of her condition had on his life. "The birth of our sister was a real blessing. My parents got so involved in promoting and fundraising in the state of Delaware. I think it had an enormous impact on me."

Way Marking

Pat's baseball skills at Tower Hill earned him a partial baseball scholarship to Wake Forest University. He was recruited by then-coach Dr. Gene Hooks. While not entirely disappointed with his physical ability as a catcher, Gene also wasn't overly impressed. Pat's knowledge of the game, however, is really where Gene saw something special in Pat. Dr. Hooks said, "It was like having a coach on the field. He was just so completely enamored with the game and so on top of everything from the strategies involved, the pitches to call, and how to hold a man on base. It was really a pleasure working with him."

"Wake Forest was the perfect school for me," Pat said before highlighting the different life paths besides baseball he traveled while enrolled there. "I really began to find myself. I had a radio sports show on the campus radio station. I wrote periodically for the school newspaper. And all the other older catchers had graduated when I enrolled, so I caught every game for four years."

Ernie Accorsi, Pat's longtime friend and former general manager of three National Football League (NFL) teams, was a student at Wake Forest with Pat. He described Pat's remarkable ability to pursue his visions, saying, "He was president of the Monogram Club. He was elected as one of the ten most outstanding seniors at Wake Forest. He was a campus leader. There was no question about it.

"He was also a very good broadcaster. He went out and sold the time and did the play-by-play of the freshman basketball games," Ernie—who was also a beat writer for the *Philadelphia Inquirer* during Pat's first year with the 76ers—said about Pat's tremendous gift in the broadcast booth. "There was a broadcaster named Andy Musser who was doing our games at the 76ers. He said, 'Pat, you're going to have to make up your mind. Do you want to be a play-by-play announcer or a general manager?' Pat had ability in both areas. He could've gone either way."

According to Wake Forest teammate and longtime National Collegiate Athletic Association (NCAA) basketball broadcaster Billy Packer, Pat's communication skills and leadership roles in college combined to produce Pat's first foray into sports promotion, saying, "Wake Forest had a freshman versus varsity basketball game, but nobody had put together the business plan for selling tickets. Pat got the assignment because it was a fundraiser for the Letterman's Club. It was the first time he got involved in sports promotion, going out to sell tickets and drumming up support. In a small way, it was the beginning of what turned out to be a great career."

Pat seemed to excel at everything he put his hands to in college but often left behind big shoes to fill. One such example was a future college football and NFL coach named John Mackovic—who was Pat's successor as president of the Letterman's Club. "I don't want to say he took me under his wing, but he was Mr. Letterman at Wake Forest," John said. Having earned his letter as a sophomore, John noticed Pat's waymaker hand on him, saying, "Every now and then we'd get together and have a meeting. He always kind of moved me along. When he graduated, he said, 'Our next person is going to be John,' and I took over that role for the next two years."

Unlike those who may enter college without a vision for their future mapped out, Pat knew the path that he wanted his college education to take. He had a degree in physical education in his sights. When recalling his early days at Wake Forest, Pat quickly learned to manage his time effectively so he wouldn't find himself off course, saying, "There were four rooms to a quad, two people in each room. That meant there were eight people in that little rooming area. I thought there was going to be a lot of noise and it would be disruptive. I learned to take my books and my assignments over to the library, where there was a deathly quiet."

Lenny Aulleto played on a summer league team with Pat in 1961. He shared about the characteristics Pat exhibited during this college season of life. He said, "My initial impression of Pat was that he was a very positive person. He would always have a pat on the back or words of encouragement. I feel fortunate that Pat passed my way while we were young college guys. Pat was always beyond his years and more mature than most of us. During these early days, he was someone who was a decent, hardworking, and—most of all—caring person."

Pat learned to block out distractions on his way to graduating from Wake Forest in June of 1962. That September, he carried that focus and determination into his grad studies at Indiana University (IU)—where he earned a master of science degree in physical education in 1964. Pat describes almost going through school with blinders on, saying, "In that period, I also learned about putting things off and procrastination. If you've got a task in front of you, if you've got an assignment, jump on it immediately, and don't wait for some magic to happen.

"In addition to working on my master's degree," Pat continued, "IU was a big turning point for me. Big campus. Big state school. The big time of college athletics. That was a big difference maker for me. I built confidence. I had a good experience. I came out of IU challenged intellectually. I had my master's before my twenty-fourth birthday."

Broadcasting was a path that Pat continued to explore while at IU, even though it had been embarked upon while he was at Wake Forest. Future Milwaukee Bucks broadcaster and NBA player Jon McGlocklin played basketball at IU while Pat was announcing their games. "Pat did the games my sophomore and junior year," Jon said. "He traveled with us and was with us a lot. Quite frankly, in my fraternity house of about 120 men, they would watch the games on TV but turn on the radio to hear Pat."

Another path Pat found himself navigating branched during his baseball career at Wake Forest, when he received a call to come to a meeting in the offices of the Philadelphia Phillies—a Major League Baseball team. Phillies then-owner Bob Carpenter, who was previously mentioned as a cofounder of the Blue-Gold All-Star Game along with Pat's father, wanted to offer Pat an opportunity.

"Are you broke?" Bob asked from his office with Pat seated across from him. "Yes," Pat replied. "Well, we'll give you $500 to sign and $400 a month. Come up to the office tomorrow, and there'll be a contract waiting for you." Pat did. The next day he was in his car driving to Florida to play professional baseball for the Miami Marlins—which was a Phillies farm club in the Florida State League.

After years of hard work and dedication to his vision, Pat's path to becoming a professional baseball player had been accomplished. Pat said, "Everything that's happened ever since, I can lay right at the feet of that season, because I got to experience the life of a professional athlete and what goes with it. The ups and the downs. The fears, the joys, and the insecurities. Everything that comes with being a pro ball player. I got to taste it, feel it, and live it."

Pat played baseball for the Phillies farm club while he was still working on his master's degree in physical education. He said, "I was not a highly rated prospect by any means, but the Phillies did give me the opportunity. That's all I ever wanted."

Even though it had been his childhood dream, after a couple of years in Miami, Pat knew his future in baseball may not be on the field. He said, "It was obvious that I was not going to go any higher. I'd reached my limit. The Phillies knew that. I knew it. But I had an intense desire to stay in baseball. That was what I loved. That's what I wanted to do. And the Phillies gave me the opportunity."

When facing a setback, many people would try to regroup. They may take time to lick their wounds or figure out what to do next. Waymakers are not often found taking steps back. That defeats the purpose of their nature to create new paths in the first place. Instead, waymakers find ways to go around obstacles in life or, in Pat's case, take the loss of his childhood dream to be a pro ball player and redirect his passion for sports onto a new path of unknown destination.

Pat was sent back to Miami as an executive to work under Bill Durney, the general manager of the Miami Marlins. Pat remembers the early days of his relationship with Bill, saying, "He had kind of taken a shine to me, and he wanted me with him in the front office for the '64 season. I was a sponge. Everything Bill Durney said. Everything he did. I watched him. I followed him. I drained every piece of baseball knowledge and experience from him that I could."

In 1965, after what proved to be a valuable internship under Bill Durney, Pat was given the general-manager job for another team in the Phillies farm system in Spartanburg, South Carolina. Pat's success in Spartanburg would lead to an unexpected offer that would change the course of Pat's life forever. ★

★ ★ ★

CHAPTER TWO

FIND A GOOD MENTOR

A Life-Changing Discovery

"I had an off day from the Miami team in July of 1962. I went downtown and ended up in a Burdines department store," Pat recalled when talking about the events that led to his early success as a professional sports executive. "There was a book that had just come out, *Veeck as in Wreck*—which were the memoirs of Bill Veeck."

Veeck was best known for being an owner of several professional baseball franchises throughout his life, including the St. Louis Browns, the Cleveland Indians, and the Chicago White Sox. As Pat began to read Veeck's book, he noticed that interspersed throughout the book was the name Bill Durney—who had been with Veeck while he was with the St. Louis Browns. Serendipitously, Bill also currently happened to be the general manager of Pat's baseball team—the Miami Marlins.

Pat went to talk with Durney about this discovery, saying, "After the season, I'm heading home to Wilmington, Delaware. I heard Bill Veeck is living in retirement an hour or so from me in Easton, Maryland. I would love to meet him. Could you help me?" "I'll take care of it," Durney replied. He caught up with Pat a week later by phone. "Veeck wants to meet you. Here's his number."

Pat remembered his first phone call and initial visit with Bill Veeck, saying, "My hands were trembling when I started to call that number. I had to redial three times. After he answered, he invited me down to his estate. It was a beautiful September day when I drove down and found him at home. He was reading and sunning himself without a shirt on his front porch. His leg was off, and he was wearing a pair of khaki shorts." Veeck—whose leg had been amputated after being smashed by an antiaircraft gun while serving in the Marines in 1943—began to chat with Pat and soon invited him to stay for lunch.

"The next thing I knew, it was four o'clock in the afternoon, and I'd been with him for close to four or five hours," Pat said before describing the impact that his initial meeting with Veeck had on the rest of his life. "That meeting was a life changer for me, because for twenty-five years, he was a friend. He was a mentor. He was an advisor. I never worked for him, but he was always there whenever I would have a question or needed something to be cleared up. I was so fortunate that he took an interest in me, and it made a huge difference in my life and my career."

Open-Door Relationships

There is a common thread among waymakers: the ability to build, maintain, and nurture many relationships. Waymakers use the trust gained from their genuine relationships to help, encourage, and influence the paths of those that are close to them. Waymakers see great value in keeping many deep and meaningful relationships, even if those relationships are only nurtured from a distance.

Pat maintains treasured relationships with people from every corner of our country, and some of those relationships only get watered every few years through phone calls or an occasional dinner. Regardless of distance or frequency of conversation, every relationship is important to Pat. Pat officially grasped this lesson of valuing every relationship when he met Bill Veeck. In Veeck, Pat found a friend and mentor who would encourage him in every aspect of his life. From then on, Pat desired to live a life doing the same for others.

"We all need people in our life who have an interest in us, who want the best for us, and who are there to open doors for us."

Pat's waymaking ways can easily be traced back through that moment in September of 1962, when he walked onto that porch with Veeck for the first time. Pat summed up the need for a great mentor best when he said, "We all need people in our life who have an interest in us, who want the best for us, and who are there to open doors for us."

Pat continued to talk about how his mentor/mentee relationship with Veeck opened up doors for his future, saying, "When I got the Chicago Bulls job at age twenty-nine, it was Bill Veeck who opened the door, because he knew a key person in the Bulls' ownership group and he was there pushing for me by phone with one of the key owners. I didn't know that was going on, but it was a huge part of how I moved from Philly after one year and went to the Chicago Bulls and became the GM. Bill was a big part of that happening. We need those people in our lives."

Pat has learned to be, for me and so many others, what Veeck was for him. A mentor. A friend. Someone who believes in you. One such example is former Magic employee Brian Kamuda, who said, "One day, I asked his assistant to schedule a lunch. I wanted to connect with him as a possible mentor because he was the guy that sold ten thousand tickets for a team and building that didn't exist. I'm not sure if it was our sense of humor, but we've been pretty well connected ever since."

After Brian left the Magic, he headed north to run an eighty-year-old family business in Vermont, where Pat continues to be an instrumental mentor in Brian's life. Brian said the advice and encouragement he has received from Pat ranges from "how to start a speech" to "name considerations he gave me for my son."

As a business owner, Brian is now leading his team and hopes to reciprocate mentorship back to those coming up behind him, like Pat did, saying, "I got to be around one of the most influential people in pro sports. Someone that truly understands leadership and could convey how to take it from conceptual to real life. He's made me a better father, a better husband, and a better business owner."

Opportunities to mentor others have come to Pat from areas outside the NBA, as well. Andy Benoit was a guest on Pat's radio show, discussing an NFL preview book he had written. "I didn't know who he was at the time," Andy recalled, but found the opportunity to get to know him better a few weeks later when Pat—who was visiting Andy's hometown of Boise, Idaho, to give a speech—invited him to be his special guest.

Andy remembers, "We were in the buffet line, and I knew he worked for the Magic, but he downplayed it." Andy later said he found out Pat was "basically running the Magic at the time." He said, "At my age, I could've been name-dropping Pat Williams all the time, but it was really cool to see how easy, fluid, and humble he was about all of that." After dinner, Pat gave a speech inside the ballroom of the Riverside Hotel that Andy called "the best speech I ever heard in my life."

The area of greatest mentoring for Andy came in the subject of reading. He said, "Pat really challenged me in that area. I probably wrote more books than I read at that point in my life. He really refocused my perception of reading. I have read thirty to ninety minutes a day on average for the rest of my life after meeting him."

Another example of someone Pat mentored to prioritize reading was Jack Elkins. "I don't tend to put myself out there very much, and Pat has been the one to inspire me to speak and take action. I was always a voracious learner, but his speeches around reading catalyzed that for me to go way over the top. My book readings over the years have increased to the point where I have become a subject matter expert on innovation and creativity."

Jack met Pat during his fifteen-year tenure with the Orlando Magic. Jack said, "In the last couple of years, [spending more quality time together] was something that helped me immensely to be able to branch out to start my own businesses. He took the type of action that he is famous for—which is giving a bit of a boost." Jack later referred to getting that needed boost of encouragement as "getting a little bit of the famous Pat Williams magic."

Waymakers know the value of relationships, but they first need to learn how to be on the receiving end of encouragement so that they can later pass similar lessons on to others. Finding a great mentor may not be an easy task, but we should always be looking for one. Not only did Pat continually seek to find a mentor of his own in Veeck, but he has continued to pay it forward by finding various ways to mentor others. ★

★ ★ ★

CHAPTER THREE

PAY ATTENTION

Capture Mode

Pat has a Rolodex memory, something I will refer to often when describing the way that he tells stories in great detail. I find it incredible each time he is able to so easily pull a name or date out of his mind when he is telling me a story from fifty years ago—it's as if each memory in his brain has been cataloged and filed away for easy retrieval later on in life.

During many of our conversations, Pat recalled with great accuracy the dates, people, and history of many of his stories. Some of you may have a hard time remembering the name of every class you took in college or the names of your childhood teachers. You may also have forgotten some of the names of your coworkers from your first job, let alone the exact dates you met them while working there decades ago. Not Pat. Those details come easy.

Pat's ability to catalog memories plays a big part in how he was able to become a waymaker for himself and others. Pat wasn't successful only because he had a good memory; he was successful because his good memory allowed him to hold on to the details that make being a waymaker possible. He knew how to distill the lessons he learned from others to create paths you and I could follow.

Fellow circuit speaker and author Don Yaeger has consistently seen Pat's memory serve his ability to speak and influence others with greater propensity, saying, "If you say, 'Today, Pat, the discussion is going to be on building mental strength,' the next thing you know, he has three or four stories and lessons. He has the close that the rest of us would love to have built, practiced, and recorded fifty times so we could be that good. Pat just does it. We all think it looks simple, but I know how difficult it is."

Pat has ways of listening to others that we could benefit from if we learn how to implement his strategies in our own lives. When someone talks to Pat, he listens intently. He always cares what the person talking to him is saying. When his mentor—or anyone he is trying to learn something from—talks, however, his listening ability goes to a higher level. I call this level *capture mode*. In capture mode, Pat will listen for the things he has never heard before. Pat is trying to capture the information the speaker is sharing that he himself doesn't already know so he can use it in his own life moving forward.

For example, when I talked to Pat about his relationship with Bill Veeck, he lovingly described his mentor as a genius of sports promotion. Pat said, "Bill was the most creative, imaginative sports executive we've ever seen. And he kept stressing to me, 'Don't be afraid to do new things. Don't be afraid to take your ideas and put them into action. Don't be reluctant to gamble, to take some risks in presenting baseball to your fans. Don't just open the park up and have a game.'"

Pat was never at a loss to describe the multitude of lessons he learned from Veeck, saying, "You've got to work hard at getting people into your ballpark. To experience it. And hope that they have such a good time that they come back again and bring their friends with them. Bill said, 'You can't control the win-and-loss column. It's too risky.' But he also said, 'You can control everything else that goes on in your ballpark.'"

In school, we might remember one or two main points from a teacher's lesson. Pat remembers almost everything.

Pat remembers the details. God has created him this way. Paying attention to details is another characteristic of a waymaker. How else can you create a map for others to follow if you can't write down the details of the trail they are going to walk on? Pat's ability to listen for the things not known, however, is perhaps the utmost lesson in paying attention we can learn in our attempt to be like Pat.

Of all the above lessons that Bill Veeck taught to Pat, which one do you think is the one Pat captured and used to lead him toward success? Was it "Don't be afraid to gamble" or "You've got to work hard to get people into your ballpark?" Or something else? What do you think was the most important lesson Bill gave Pat? Do you even remember what they all were?

During conversations, many of us may drown out or forget large chunks of what is being said. In school, we might remember one or two main points from a teacher's lesson. Pat remembers almost everything. Therefore, he is able to look for things unknown to him, capture them, and apply them to his life. While listening to Bill Veeck, the most important lesson Pat captured was a phrase Veeck used but that he had never heard before—"You can't control the win-and-loss column, but you can control everything else that goes on in your ballpark."

35

All the other lessons Pat learned from Bill may have been valuable, but his ability to remember them all so that he could sort out the best one is what makes Pat special. Pat immediately took the lesson of ignoring the standings inside the paper while focusing on the fans inside the ballpark into his newfound career of professional sports management.

Applying What He Learned

Pat's first general-manager job was for a Phillies minor-league club in Spartanburg, South Carolina. He immediately put his focus toward making the ballpark as important as the team that was playing in it. Pat said, "I was there four years, learning and running my own team. And it was a marvelous experience. The Phillies sent some good young players. We had success on the field, which was certainly helpful, and we promoted up a storm. Anything we could do to get people in the ballpark that was clean and legal and moral, we did it."

Bobby Malkmus was the manager at Spartanburg that year. He remembers Pat being "a go-getter," adding, "Pat had a lot of life to him. He was always experimenting with new things to promote the game of baseball." One of those experiments included a night where Bobby said, "All the bald people would come into the ballpark for nothing, and they would receive a comb."

MLB scout Gary Nichols has worked in baseball for more than fifty years. His first job was with the Phillies organization while Pat was the general manager in Spartanburg. After meeting for the first time in one of the club boxes, Gary began to notice Pat's demeanor, saying, "You can't help but be influenced by his enthusiasm and joy of working in sports and to be able to do something that you really love rather than just work."

In Spartanburg, Pat worked for team owner R. E. Littlejohn. He remarked that Mr. R. E. "was so much more than an owner. He was a mentor to me. A great friend." Littlejohn showed his trust in Pat to do the job while also allowing him to run the promotions and spend the budget how he saw fit, which would not have been a normal occurrence for owners of these lower-level teams.

Murray Cook was a player and general manager of the nearby Gastonia Pirates in the since-defunct Western Carolinas League. Murray explained how Pat's promotions weren't a natural part of the baseball experience for teams during that period, saying, "Managers just tried to maintain the status quo. You really didn't do much promoting. Pat's ideas were ahead of their time, but he also worked for a guy that would let him do those things."

Under Pat's leadership, the ballpark in Spartanburg set new attendance records. The success in Spartanburg, which stemmed in part from Pat implementing philosophies from his mentor Bill Veeck, got the attention of other owners, including some in other sports. A call from Jack Ramsay in July of 1968 led to an unpredictable turning point in Pat's sports career.

Pat said, "Jack explained to me he was out in California concluding the trade that was sending Wilt Chamberlain to the Lakers. He also told me that he needed somebody to run the front office because he was going to be the new full-time coach. He was calling because he wanted to talk to me about that position.

"I was stunned," Pat continued to say about the call that would steer his career in a new direction for the next fifty years. After several interviews, Pat accepted the job in the NBA as business manager of the Philadelphia 76ers. Pat was aware that his new path was an extreme departure from a whole life enveloped by baseball, saying, "Baseball had been my entire focus. I was twenty-eight years old, switching sports, but it was the first opportunity I received to get to a big-league sports city."

An overwhelmed yet confident Pat was determined to take the lessons he learned in baseball and apply them to the NBA. His first goal was to learn whether the advice from Bill Veeck to ignore the standings and focus on the fans in the ballpark would translate from baseball to basketball, as well as from the minor leagues to the professional ones.

Pat said, "I bought into that. I believed it all the way through to today. And when I had an opportunity to leave and go to the big leagues of sports in Philadelphia, it was not baseball. I had heard that the things I was doing down in the minor leagues were fine, but they weren't going to play in the big leagues, in the big cities. I was determined to find out."

The budgets for promotions Pat had in Philadelphia were quite larger than the ones he'd had in Spartanburg, but the goal was still to find new ways to entertain people while at the game. This philosophy is likely what created early success in Pat's career. He wasn't focused on whether the team was winning; he couldn't control that. He focused on the fans. Pat said his main concern was "Were the fans having a good time at the game whether the team won or lost?"

Pat remembered what it was like during his first year in the NBA, saying, "I took all that I had learned from Bill Veeck and the experiences in Spartanburg, and I took them to Philadelphia and put them to work. As that year went on, I became convinced that it doesn't matter the size of the city. People are the same. They want to go to an event. They want to see a good game. They want to have a good time. They want it to be a fun evening. And if they had enough of a good time, they want to come back."

Pat's increased budget, however, did lead to some pretty interesting promotions during his first year in the NBA. Some of the promotions seen by 76ers fans during Pat's inaugural season included Victor the Wrestling Bear, a popular singing group name led by the Phils' Dick Allen, called the Ebonistics—who sang their hit "Echoes of November"—and a trained pig act called Uncle Heavy's Pork Chop Review.

Tim Malloy worked for the 76ers with Pat and knows how hard it was to fill seats and get people to watch basketball on TV in the early years of the NBA. He said, "The Finals in '80 and '81 were on tape delay. Nobody would take the ratings. We played the Milwaukee Bucks in a playoff game in front of, like, nine thousand people. That's unheard of now."

Tim went on to describe more of the differences that Pat navigated in the NBA during his early career versus today, saying, "We used to get two seats each as an employee. They were worth $11 and were right behind the bench. Now that seat is probably $200. Front row seats, I don't think they existed when we were there. At least not at the price of $2,500 apiece, like they are now." Tim finished by adding, "You needed to grind to get people in the seats, and Pat was brilliant at it."

NBA Hall of Famer Oscar Robertson met Pat around the time he was traded from the Cincinnati Royals to the Milwaukee Bucks and described how Pat's initial promotions caused some to think he was going to upset the applecart. Oscar said, "Some people liked his ideas and some didn't, but he was on top of everything. He knew the game. He knew people. Those two combinations made him very successful."

In Pat's early days as a basketball executive, the NBA was not producing the $8 billion in revenue it does today. Pat's early promotions, however, helped fill arenas that previously couldn't sell out seats at bedrock prices. Many see Pat's performance as a promotional powerhouse as the factor that helped steer the NBA toward becoming a large-scale revenue generator.

Years later, Pat continually paid attention to things that would help fill seats in his arenas. While out in Los Angeles, California, on a book tour with publicist Ken Wilson, Pat visited the Forum for an LA Lakers game. During the game, Ken recalled Pat "being more interested in talking to the fans who were sitting around when there was a break in the action. He asked the people behind us, 'How often do you come to Lakers games?' They said, 'Not often because it is expensive.'" Ken compared Pat's interviews to market research questions. Pat would ask, "Let's see, what gets people out to Lakers games? Is it the same thing that gets people to come out to an Orlando Magic game?"

After his first year in the NBA, Pat proved that Veeck's lesson to control things at the ballpark worked at any level. Pat continued throughout his career to utilize his waymaker ability to pay attention and listen for the things not known, saying, "My Veeck training worked. First in Philadelphia, then Chicago, then Atlanta, then back to Philadelphia, and the last thirty-plus years here in Orlando. And now we're attempting to bring major league baseball here. And it'll be done, if we get the team, with the same amount of flare that I learned from Bill. You can't beat fun at the old ballpark." ★

★ ★ ★

CHAPTER FOUR

FIND FAITH IN CHRIST

Church and Pancakes

"I never questioned the existence of God. I just never thought about it," Pat said in our first long discussion about Christianity. While Pat's strong faith in Jesus was the main reason I was drawn to tell his story, it took time to become a priority in his life. Today, however, Pat Williams's name has become synonymous with Christianity. His faith in Christ is a predominant reason Pat has truly become a meaningful waymaker. Pat's best man and founder of the Dallas Mavericks, Norm Sonju, stated the importance of Pat's faith to me most concisely when he said, "If you miss Pat's faith, you really miss him."

Pat's grandfather was a pastor in Greensboro, North Carolina. Pat's father, however, was not a church attender. Instead, it was his mother who took Pat and his sisters to church every Sunday through his last year of high school.

At Wake Forest—the Baptist state school of North Carolina at the time—Pat continued to be surrounded by the teachings of Christ. "They had required chapel twice a week, and you had to attend. They had, as a part of the curriculum, a couple of religion courses you had to take. And that was pretty much the extent of it," Pat said about his mandatory faith training at college.

Curious by nature, Pat seemed to have an uncharacteristically small number of questions or thoughts about religion or faith throughout his school years. He said, "It didn't penetrate. It didn't do much for me. I had no spiritual leanings at all." Although Don Roth—who was both Pat's roommate and battery mate on the baseball field for three years at Wake Forest—shared a story about how they spent some of their Sundays together searching for a spiritual home. "Pat was a Presbyterian. I was a Lutheran. We had a friend who was a Catholic and a friend who was a Baptist."

Don continued, "We decided to go to a different church every Sunday, just to see where we would like to attend. First, we went to the one on the campus, which was a Baptist chapel at the time. The next week, we went to another one, and we went to another one and another one." No spiritual answers were found on this J. R. R. Tolkien–type fellowship quest, however, because when I asked Don which church they'd decided to go to, he said, "Well, we ended up going to the one that had a free pancake breakfast!"

Lifting the Veil

Pat said his first big step down the road toward a relationship with Christ came while he was the GM of the Spartanburg Phillies in South Carolina. "I was right there in the middle of the Bible Belt, surrounded by Christians, including the owner of the team—R. E. Littlejohn—and his family. They never preached to me. I did see something in their life that was different, but I never really discussed that with them."

On the heels of the team's enormous success in Spartanburg, God began to open the eyes of Pat in some unique ways. The first of several eye-opening moments, Pat said, that led to his salvation—which are laid out in greater detail in his biography called *Ahead of the Game*—started in the spring of 1967.

Pat shared, "It was my third year in Spartanburg. I had a promotion where I brought in a fellow named Paul Anderson, who carried the nickname 'the Strongest Man in the World.' Paul raised money for

> I was confused when he wrote 'Your friend in Christ.' I'd never seen anything like that. I didn't know really what it meant."

his youth home in Vidalia, Georgia, by going out and speaking and demonstrating his feats of strength. After he did those feats of strength in the ballpark one night, he addressed the crowd and said, 'I may be the strongest man in the world, but I can't get through a minute of the day without Jesus Christ in the centerpiece of my life.'"

After their initial meeting in Spartanburg, Paul signed a picture for Pat before he left that said, "To Pat, your friend in Christ, Paul Anderson." Pat recalled being a little confused by Paul's actions, saying, "Well, the crowd there gave him a nice response. I heard what he said, but I didn't really grasp it. I was impressed with him and liked him, but I was confused when he wrote 'your friend in Christ.' I'd never seen anything like that. I didn't know really what it meant."

Paul's wife, Glenda Anderson, now runs the Paul Anderson Youth Home, since Paul went to be with the Lord in 1994. Pat has still remained close to that organization—which works with young men who would otherwise be incarcerated. Glenda said about Pat, "He is a giver. He's very interested in people. I think he's a connector. He knows everybody, and if he thinks that someone can help someone, he puts them in touch with each other."

Pat's initial interaction with Paul was one of a few distinguishing moments that finally sparked the inquisitive nature Pat normally displays when he is interested in learning more about something. The more successes he saw in his career, the louder the questions in his mind began to get. Pat said, "I noticed that there was no ultimate filling of the inner core of my being. There was an emptiness there, and I tried to fill it with success, fame, and, to a certain degree, fortune. I was single. I enjoyed my life as a single bachelor. But there remained this question: 'Is this all there is to life?' It was gnawing at me." Those small—but large—events of God leading Pat to Him finally culminated in February of 1968.

After attending a basketball game at a nearby sports center, Pat found himself in an auditorium where a traveling singing group was performing a concert consisting mostly of folk songs. Pat remembered, "They took an intermission and said, 'When we come back, we want to talk to you about what the Lord means in our lives.'

"When they came back, their songs were centered on a Savior," Pat continued. "A little blond girl was one of the singers and introduced herself as Sandy Johnson. After the show ended, I made my way to the front and introduced myself. Before I left, she handed me a booklet called *Four Spiritual Laws*."

Pat said, "When I got home, I worked my way through this little book—which pointed out the four different aspects about knowing that God loves you and you've got a sin problem. And this man Jesus died for your sin problem, and to fully experience that, you've got to invite Him into your life." After finally finding some real answers to questions he had on his heart, Pat decided to reach out to the only person he could think of for help—Sandy Johnson.

After locating the singing group at a local motel, Pat called Sandy's room and asked to meet. The next morning at a restaurant across from the group's motel, Pat asked Sandy to explain the gospel message of the book in detail. "She did," he said, recalling the whirlwind moments of this chance encounter. "She explained it all to me." Pat remembered thinking, "This is not all that complicated. I always thought that anything pertaining to Christianity was just too confusing and unfathomable except for the select few. But she pointed it out and taught me very clearly."

A few moments later, Sandy was on a bus heading out of town to play the next show. Still curious and a bit confused about what he just learned, Pat reached out to another Christian he knew in town—R. E. Littlejohn, the owner of the Spartanburg Phillies. "What's happening to me?" Pat asked, after locating and meeting with the man he referred to as a surrogate father.

"Pat, the Lord is working on you, and He wants you. And now is the time to make this decision," Mr. Littlejohn said. "You've been reading about it. You've been hearing about it. It's time." At that moment Pat recalled that he melted, saying, "I collapsed on his shoulder in tears, deep tears, way-down tears. And he just held me and talked very quietly about the work that God could do in my life.

"Eventually, I stood up, and my tears dried, and I knew then that something very dramatic had happened," Pat said about his life-altering moment. "I felt completely cleansed on the inside. I felt that all my sinful past had been wiped out, had been forgiven. And I felt that there was a new purpose in my life. I was an instant conversion. I suddenly had a new focus, a new direction in life. I knew then that God was going to do something in my life that I could never have done myself. I felt that I had surrendered to Him and that I was in His hands now." ★

CHAPTER FIVE

TRUST GOD

Letting Go of the Wheel

Having faith in Christ for salvation and trusting God to guide your future are two separate acts. Even after becoming born again, Pat wasn't exactly confident where his future was headed. He did, however, have confidence in who held his future. Pat had faith for salvation but was now learning to put his trust in God to guide his path.

Trust is a foundational lesson of becoming a waymaker, because you often walk down unmarked trails. Finding the correct way out of those trails without becoming lost can be difficult. Putting your trust in God to lead the way out instead of trying to find your own is one way to distinguish yourself as a waymaker instead of a trailblazer.

Initially, Pat questioned if he would be able to actually let go of the wheel and let God drive, saying, "Now, the big issue at this point was, had I really taken my hands off of my life. Particularly, had I taken them off my career, where I would not be maneuvering and trying to move up the ladder, to elevate myself in the sports world and get to the next levels. Would I be willing and able to completely remove my hands from my life and my baseball career?"

He continued, "I prayed that I would. I also felt that it was happening. I really felt comfortable. I remember thinking, 'If I end up staying in Spartanburg, South Carolina, the rest of my life, if that's what the Lord wants, I'm fine with that. That's the way it'll be.'"

Pat, of course, didn't stay in baseball. Instead, his early career had two major pathfinder opportunities available—which required him to make life-changing choices. The first was made out of Pat's own desire to continue a path in pro sports after his playing days were over. The other was a call by God to switch from the comfort of the baseball world to the foreign courts of basketball.

Pat believed God was directing his path toward basketball because he hadn't previously made any maneuver to go in that direction. The call was completely unexpected. Pat said, "I had told God that my hands were off my life. I was going to let Him handle it. And He did. In a way I never could have imagined."

Passing On Opportunities

Right before Pat started working with the Philadelphia 76ers basketball team, he received another unexpected call from Jim Fanning. Fanning—whom Pat knew from the world of major league baseball—was working with another man named John McHale to run a brand-new expansion team called the Montreal Expos. On the call, Fanning said, "Pat, we'd like you to join us and make it a trio."

Pat's boyhood dream of running an MLB franchise was suddenly right in front of him. Pat prayed and thanked the Lord for such an amazing opportunity. He could hardly believe that getting out of God's way would bring such riches of opportunity. The moment was short lived, however, because a mixture of discernment and integrity wouldn't allow Pat to follow down this other new path. Pat told Jim, "I am so honored, so flattered, but I just signed a deal to go to work for the 76ers. I start work Monday morning. I am so sorry."

Waymakers will often be put at the feet of new opportunities. It can be difficult for them to decide which trail is best when their nature is to walk down many paths. It is because of this nature that trusting God is so important to the lives of waymakers. In the Bible, Ephesians 2:10 tells us we were created to do good things God designed in advance for us to do. If God knows the best path for us to take, shouldn't we consult Him to find it?

On more than one occasion, Pat would be faced with opportunities to leave the NBA and fulfill his childhood dream to manage a Major League Baseball team. "I interviewed with the Orioles twice," Pat said, "early into my NBA career and then again in 1973 when it was time to leave the Bulls. The Orioles called and offered me the GM post over the phone. I just didn't feel comfortable accepting it because, at the same time, there was an offer to become the GM of the Atlanta Hawks. And I had been in the NBA at that point for five years. I was enjoying my time in pro basketball immensely, and I just felt that that's the path I should follow."

Pat took his hands off the wheel of his career. Opportunities soon followed. Pat's relationship with Christ allowed him to hear from God and to follow His voice—which are two key ingredients to making choices that define an Ephesians 2:10 life. While it wasn't necessarily easy for him, Pat was able to successfully determine which career paths were correct to take.

Pat retired from an enormously successful career in the NBA fifty-one years later, and he puts his trust in God at center stage as the reason for his career successes, saying, "God set it up. God made sure that it happened. And I still stand in amazement at what happens when you surrender to the Lord and turn your life over to Him. I didn't seek any of this out, but God kept opening those doors, and I was able to walk through them. And when we trust Him totally with our life and our career, He makes the way for us. I'm a firm believer in that." ★

CHAPTER SIX

CHASE A BIG VISION

A New Challenge

Chasing a big vision starts with having a vision. Pat Williams, of course, has never lacked in this area. Since he was a child, Pat has chased a career in professional sports. After achieving that goal, he chased visions to improve the various teams he was hired to work for. While in the NBA, Pat chased and caught visions to run marathons, write over one hundred books, adopt children from four foreign countries, and finish reading one book a day.

Of course, the biggest and most notable of Pat's captured visions was founding the Orlando Magic. After spending twelve years as the GM of the Philadelphia 76ers, Pat said, "I could have stayed in Philly, but I had grown very restless. I needed a new challenge. We had been to the NBA Finals four times and had won the title in 1983."

Upon deciding he was ready for a new challenge, Pat determined that "the greatest challenge in the sports world is expansion." He said, "I caught the expansion bug. One of the people who helped fuel that was Norm Sonju. My dear friend, and good Christian brother, had started an expansion team in Dallas. He was the architect of the Dallas Mavericks, and I remember spending a good amount of time talking with him about moving to Orlando and taking a shot in the dark. Norm kept encouraging me. He said, 'If you can pull it off, the rewards will be out of this world. If it fails, you can always get another job.'"

Pat continued, "So we took a big gulp and moved to Orlando in June of 1986. I was forty-six years old when we moved, and at the time Orlando was really a rather small market. No skyline. Dumpy airport. No Universal Studios. Disney was here, but nothing like the Disney of today. My job was to rally the community and sell the NBA that we could do it here."

After landing in Orlando, Pat began meeting leaders in the community. He also started building his team. Jack Swope—who first worked with Pat in the Sixers organization—was part of the small team Pat assembled after the NBA granted Orlando a franchise in 1987. Jack said, "I can remember when we had our first little staff meeting. It was above a deli, and it was just an office space that one of the minority owners had. There were six of us, I think, in there. Pat called us into our little staff meeting, and we're sitting around a fireplace. He said, 'These are going to probably be some of the best times we'll ever have.'

"In some ways, he was right," Jack said, "because we were all so intimately involved in every step of the way, and everyone knew what each other was doing. When we won the NBA championship in 1983, and I look at the picture of not just the team but the front-office staff, and there's like thirty people. When I left the Magic, it was like two hundred people."

"Other cities wanted [into the league] as well," Pat said. "Miami, Charlotte, Minnesota, Toronto, and Anaheim. They all wanted in, and we didn't know what was going to happen. It was going to be extremely competitive. So I began running around Orlando, saying, 'Folks, we need one-hundred-dollar deposits on season tickets so that we can show the NBA that our community wants to do this.'"

Sid Cash said, "Pat came up with this idea. We needed to sell ten thousand season tickets." Sid—who was a banker and salesman in the Orlando area prior to Pat's arrival—used his local connections. "I got him into some clubs," Sid said. "He worked tirelessly to pitch that idea." Jack Swope was there and remembers "coming down and going on the rubber-chicken circuit. Going over to speak to the Kiwanis Clubs and places like that."

While optimistic, Pat realized the challenge he faced in selling season tickets. He said, "The problem was there had never been a major league sport team here in Orlando. It certainly was also not a basketball area. No history at all. Plus, there was no arena to show people."

If someone were to ask, "Where are my seats going to be?" Pat would answer with "We don't know, sir. All I can tell you is that I can picture it now: it's opening night in 1988 or '89, and the Boston Celtics are in town. It's going to be the biggest game ever, and you're on the outside of the window of the arena, pounding on the door, saying, 'I can't get in. I need tickets.' I'll say, 'Do you remember three years ago when I came to your Rotary Club and I said, "Put in a deposit?" You didn't listen, did you? Now it's too late. I can't get you in, sir.'" Before closing his sale with "You don't want that to happen. Do you, folks?"

Pat's vision to bring an expansion team to Orlando was never a slam dunk idea. Jack Swope shared, "There was still a faction that said 'basketball would never work in Orlando because it was football country.' I remember people saying to Pat, 'Are you sure this is going to work here?' Pat is the eternal optimist. I always call him 'the Music Man' because Pat can just march down the road, get people going and excited. People just follow him."

> "Pat is the eternal optimist. I always call him 'the Music Man' because Pat can just march down the road, get people going and excited. People just follow him."

Jacob Stuart was relatively new at Orlando's chamber of commerce when Pat announced his intentions to bring the Magic to the city. He said, "We took a sleepy little chamber of commerce that had been borrowing money to meet payroll. We galvanized and mobilized support to make our community safer, more secure, and prosperous. The point of inflection was engaging with Pat Williams and mobilizing the chamber to lead America in the number-one ticket drive in the history of the NBA."

"Jacob Stuart and I met Pat at the same time," said Jane Hames, who was on the executive committee of the chamber. "You're instantly drawn to the guy. He's knowledgeable. He always has a handle on the facts, numbers, dates, and names. I was instantly struck by that." Jane then spoke about the growth of the city of Orlando: "It was the '80s, when everything was popping around here. We called it 'the land of the superlatives' for a while, because every day there was an announcement about the newest, biggest, or tallest hotel, restaurant, bar, or whatever. It was a lot. He came along at a time to just capture that excitement about Orlando."

While Pat's vision certainly led to a deep impact on the community, in the cases of Jacob, Jane, and so many others involved, Pat did the same for them. Jacob said, "Pat taught me you can run and train every single day and build your muscles and endurance. You can even go a couple times a week and still become a healthier individual. That is exactly what a community does. It builds civic muscle. So a victory in one way—which could be chasing an NBA franchise—gives us the momentum to later champion children who are in need."

Jacob added, "People say we're just championing millionaires and their dreams. Millionaires have a role in professional sports, and so does the community. The millionaire cannot get to the NBA Finals or the World Series without the community. The community cannot get there without the wealth of the ownership team. It's a partnership. Pat was able to have a foot in both worlds."

Launching the Vision

Pat learned valuable lessons about big vision waymaking while taking his first steps in Orlando. He said, "I think that whole experience taught me more about vision and leadership than anything that had ever happened. I was selling this vision of this team that did not exist in a league that had not committed to adding more teams. To a city that had no history of major league sports, and we didn't have any place to play. Now we had something on the come, but there was no place to show people."

He continued, "Eventually over three months, fourteen thousand deposits came in, and we were able to go to the league and say, 'Look what we've got. Look what's going on. Can you believe this?' They were very impressed. So I think in that ninety-day period, I learned so much about having a vision, communicating it, selling it." Eventually, Pat's vision and hard work paid off. He said, "We were successful in that endeavor. In April of 1987, they awarded a franchise to this little city in Florida—which is no longer a little city."

While excited that his vision to launch a team in Orlando had been successful, the work transitioned from sharing the vision to building it. John Gabriel was part of the first executive team Pat built in Orlando. John, like several other executives brought on, had worked with Pat in Philadelphia. In fact, Pat had invited so many executives from his 76ers team to join him in Orlando that people started referring to the team as the "76ers South."

John spoke about the work that went into building the team after it was awarded, saying, "This was '87. We didn't start until 1989. For two years, we had to pick the team colors and the mascot, find a coach, find a practice facility, design the floor, design the sky boxes. Six of us were intricately involved in almost every aspect of putting the team together."

Before they landed on a dragon named Stuff as a mascot and silver and blue as the team's colors, there was a major choice to make—the team name. While selling season tickets, the team was referred to as the Orlando Limited. The story of the Magic team name involves a car ride with Pat and his then-seven-year-old daughter Karyn exploring Orlando a year earlier in 1986.

Karyn was in town visiting her father prior to the family moving to the city some time later. Pat and his daughter were discussing what the team name could be. "What about Orlando Oranges?" Pat offered as one of his many ideas. From the back seat, Karyn said, "This place is magic; maybe we could name the team that." That phrase stuck with Pat, and the team now had found its name.

Nick Anderson—who was the first draft pick of the Orlando Magic in 1989—said, "Coming from Chicago, most people didn't know who the Magic were." When Nick told his friends that he was drafted by Orlando, he said, "They had never heard of them. They didn't even think it was a pro team."

Nick went on to become the Magic's most tenured player, spending a decade with the team. He played on the team's championship run in 1993 but was also able to witness Pat helping lead the team from humble beginnings to a billion-dollar franchise. Nick said, "When we started, we practiced in a recreation center right there in the neighborhood, but it was laying the foundation."

Later, Nick said, "Pat, along with ownership, built a $50 million practice facility in the new arena. That's a really big step to go from the rec center to the RDV facility." Today, Nick is thankful for the opportunity to come and start something new in Orlando. He said, "Being part of the foundation, so to speak, the first brick that was laid. That's history. It's an honor. Not many can say, 'I was the first to something being put together.'"

Reggie Theus was also a part of the inaugural season with the Magic. Reggie said, "I was the second expansion player drafted on that team. So I watched Pat orchestrate and became part of his machinery in terms of marketing. His enthusiasm. His attitude. It's infectious." He continued, "The real brilliant people in this world see things completely different. They see things in a much-further-down-the-road mentality. They can take the most minute piece of something and turn it into something much larger. To me, that has always been Pat Williams."

Sports agent Keith Glass has conducted numerous deals with Pat over the years. He saw firsthand the influence Pat had on the construction of the team, even after it was in the league. He said, "The idea of building a franchise from scratch in the middle of Florida as an expansion team was insane. He not only pulled it off, but they're thriving down there. His influence, to me, has gone way beyond being a general manager or a scout or even a president of an NBA franchise."

Magic Moments

In 2016, ESPN released a *30 for 30* documentary film highlighting the story of the Orlando Magic called *This Magic Moment*. Within the first two minutes, you are introduced to a video of a mustached Pat Williams during the early days of the team. A present-day Pat—along with many others featured in this book—then weaves the story of how pro basketball came to be in Orlando over the backdrop of images and footage from the late '80s.

Orlando news reporter Greg Warmoth was one of those featured in the film. He shared how the community was so excited for a pro team that in 1989 the station covered on the evening news the arrival at the airport of the visiting Detroit Pistons for their first exhibition game.

For this book, Greg remembered the first time he saw Pat: "It was his first day in Orlando, and he was wearing an orange shirt that said 'On our way to the NBA.' I followed that story all the way through. Followed his ticket pursuit and the building of the Orlando arena downtown to the drafting of players to the hiring of coaches and front-office personnel. I really made it my passion."

One of the big stories from Magic history—which was also covered at great length in the documentary—were the miracles surrounding the draft lottery. After a few seasons of dismal records usually associated with start-up expansion teams—which included a seventeen-game losing streak in the '91–'92 season—the Magic were certainly in the running to secure the number-one draft pick in the 1992 draft. The prize of that year would be future Hall of Famer Shaquille O'Neal.

The NBA Draft is done by a lottery that is weighted toward the teams with the worst records from the previous season. The 1992 draft was televised and showcased twelve teams. NBA commissioner David Stern would flip over oversize cards featuring a team logo, the card representing the order in which each team would slot in the upcoming draft. A representative from each team was seated at a nearby table and was shown reacting to the drama of learning their team's fate. Pat represented Orlando.

"You could feel the tension in that room," Pat said when the top two slots remained to be filled in by either Orlando or Charlotte respectively. Commissioner Stern revealed Charlotte would pick second. Pat could be heard excitedly saying, "Are you kidding me?" as he went up to take photos with the commissioner. The Orlando Magic had secured the number-one pick. That night, Pat held up a jersey labeled with the name O'Neal and the number one that the team had prepared in advance in the hope they would win that night's top prize.

The citizens of Orlando were not the only people watching the draft lottery that night. MLB Hall of Fame pitcher Fergie Jenkins was also shocked to see Pat on television as he tuned in to see which NBA team would land Shaquille. Fergie said, "Pat was my first catcher in 1962, when I was eighteen years old playing in Miami, Florida, for the Phillies organization." Fergie and Pat were teammates in 1962 and '63 but lost touch after Pat left baseball.

Fergie said, "I was really surprised to know that he had gotten out of the game, and I wasn't sure in what capacity he had stayed in sports, and I didn't know that he had become an executive in basketball until I saw him on television." Eventually reconnected, Fergie says Pat "always brings up that he had the opportunity to catch [for] a Hall of Famer and didn't know it."

After the official drafting and signing of Shaquille O'Neal—who was more commonly referred to as Shaq—the Magic improved in both record and visibility as Shaq became not only a basketball superstar but a pop-culture phenomenon. In his first season, Shaq helped the Magic improve their record by twenty games in and won

Rookie of the Year honors. Their improved record, however, also made it unlikely they would secure the following year's top draft pick.

"We had almost zero chance, when you think about it," Pat said about the Magic's chances of winning the NBA Draft lottery again in 1993. He continued, "Sixty-six ping-pong balls rolling around in this machine, and only one had the Magic logo on it." The 1993 Draft Lottery was again televised, with Pat Williams as the Orlando representative, seated a few feet from David Stern as he again flipped over cards featuring team logos. Stern revealed the Magic logo and exclaimed, "Believe it or not. The first pick in the 1993 NBA Draft goes to the Orlando Magic."

> **"We had almost zero chance, when you think about it. Sixty-six ping-pong balls rolling around in this machine, and only one had the Magic logo on it."**

"Unbelievable," NBC announcer Bob Costas reaffirmed, as the Magic beat the odds to again be the number-one pick. "That little ping-pong ball did his job and fought all the way through those sixty-five other enemies," Pat said in the documentary. In my first interview with Pat in 2017, he reflected on the results of winning both draft lotteries, saying, "The league wasn't real happy with us at that point, but I felt God wanted good things for us. That was a wonderful gift that He provided. It allowed Shaq and Penny to hook up for a number of years, and we had some really good success."

Greg Warmoth remembers, "I don't think anyone was surprised for the first one. They just thought that was Pat Williams. But the second time they won the draft lottery and got Penny Hardaway it actually changed the way the draft is done now." He added, "Many people say, if Orlando didn't have the ping-pong balls bounce their way, we would have never had success. I don't believe that, because Pat Williams would've built a championship team either way."

Pat continued to be the face of the Magic and a fixture at the televised NBA Draft lottery. The Magic picked first again in 2004 and selected Dwight Howard—who later led the team's run to the NBA Finals during the 2008–2009 season. In 2013, Pat and the Orlando Magic stood runner-up to the Cleveland Cavaliers owner Dan Gilbert's son Nick as the Cavs won the lottery—ironically with a smaller percentage chance of winning than the Magic had. The victory robbed Pat of winning the lottery for a record fourth time. Most recently, Pat unretired unofficial team mascot and former Nike endorsement character Lil' Penny—a doll based on former player Penny Hardaway—and used it as both a good luck charm and promotional gimmick when the Magic were in the running for another top selection in 2018.

Pat chasing a vision to launch a team in Orlando opened up opportunities for these stories—and many others throughout this book. Pat took a risk, but in the process found perhaps his life's most meaningful work. Today, he has spent more years living and working in Florida than any other area of the country, including the areas of Delaware and Philadelphia, where he grew up and worked.

Through the Magic, Pat helped usher in rapid and sustained growth in the city of Orlando. Countless jobs, careers, families, businesses, and nonprofits have been directly or indirectly impacted in a positive way because of his faith to flesh out a vision from God to try to start the team.

While we will touch more on his legacy later in this book, the results of Pat's vision-chasing should not go underreported. The city of Orlando and the more than seventy-five million tourists who visit each year enjoy the resources and benefits of what the city offers in part to Pat's fulfilled vision. While Pat may not have millions of followers on social media, millions of people have followed Pat to Orlando. ★

CHAPTER SEVEN

HUMBLE YOURSELF

I'm Not Famous

Pat has a storied career as a founder and general manager of multiple NBA teams. He led the Philadelphia 76ers to an NBA championship in 1983. He was an orchestrator of multiple NBA trades and drafts that significantly shaped the landscape of the sport. He also helped found the Orlando Magic in 1989.

In addition to his career, Pat has raised nineteen children, run fifty-eight marathons, climbed Mount Rainier, and even finds time to host three weekly radio shows. He is also a highly sought-after public speaker who has been asked to speak at thousands of events. Multiple halls of fame have inducted Pat into their membership, including the Naismith Memorial Basketball Hall of Fame—which awarded Pat with the John W. Bunn lifetime achievement award in 2012. The list of Pat's life and career achievements is long and continues to grow.

Prior to writing this book, my knowledge of the significance of Pat's life or work in the NBA was limited. I knew only some of the highlights. It was only when I began reaching out to friends, colleagues, and family members in Pat's life that the details of his tenure inside pro sports and his life of serving others began to emerge. Those details added more bright colors to an already beautiful portrait of Pat's life highlight reel.

Dwight Bain, Pat's longtime friend in Orlando and founder of LifeWorks Counseling Services, talked to me at great length about his friend Pat one afternoon. He recalled their most recent lunch at a local sports bar and grill. While there, Dwight described that Pat was approached by several people wanting to "get a picture and tell Pat about their first Orlando Magic game."

Dwight continued, "And then they went back to their seat with their picture to post on Instagram, and Pat said, 'I don't know why people do that.' And I looked at him and said, 'This is one of the things I love about you the most: you're really famous and you really don't care.'"

Within the NBA world, and especially in Florida, Pat Williams is well known. Not only famous, but beloved. During months of interviews, no one I talked to had either a bad word to say about Pat or an unpleasant memory to share.

Dwight went on to tell me more about Pat's level of fame and how Pat sees himself: "He just doesn't care. He doesn't pay attention to things like that. He doesn't think that way. I've seen him for over thirty years in lots of different situations, and I've just never seen him care about being famous. He does not. When we were at lunch, Pat told me, 'I'm not famous.' I replied by saying, 'Some people would say you are because you're the guy that drafted Charles Barkley. You're the guy that drafted Shaq. You're the guy who brought Kobe Bryant's dad to the Sixers, and you were there when Kobe was born.' Some people would say that's famous, but not Pat."

When Pat was new to Orlando and sharing his vision for the Magic with others, he hit it off with a man named Jim Henry. At the time, Jim was the pastor of First Baptist Orlando. The church, Jim said, "had just relocated to a new campus of 150 acres. I think Pat saw that God had blessed that and felt that 'if God could do that, He could also put a basketball team in Orlando.'"

Jim continued, "We became friends. His family joined the church, and I've had the joy of walking with him since the mid-'80s." Jim laughed as he recalled Pat and his children coming to service each week, saying, "They would come in and fill up about two rows at church. They'd come filing in, and then here comes Pat. Two rows on the right side. The whole Williams clan was going to be over there."

From those early days surrounding the birth of the Magic to Pat's idea of bringing Major League Baseball to Orlando in the form of the Dreamers, Jim has always noticed the vision and importance of how Pat sees the world, saying, "He has a faith in God that keeps him anchored and tethered." He added, "At the same time, his vision is a thing that challenges people. People want to get behind big dreamers and people with big ideas. Pat believes we have a big God so we ought to think big."

Pat's big faith, notoriety, and friendship likely played a factor when Jim allowed Pat to preach for him at First Baptist Orlando and their thousands of members while Jim acted as interim pastor at a downtown church. More likely, however, was Pat's waymaker ability to stay humble in the midst of success. Even in a crowded church of fifteen thousand members, Pat stood out as a recognizable face. Pat, however, never seemed to notice.

Jim Henry's son-in-law, Danny DeArmas—who is currently the senior associate pastor at First Baptist Orlando—said, "There are several million people in central Florida, and Pat sticks out. It's not hard for Pat to be a presence. He's just a very compelling personality."

Like Dwight Bain, Jim Henry, and so many others, Danny also realizes how the success of fulfilled visions has not brought Pat to see himself at a high level of self-importance. Danny said, "At church, Pat doesn't play the fame card or anything like that. He just acts like another one of the church members. He blends in with everybody else and shakes hands. He interacts with other people like everybody else. He doesn't have a special parking place or a special seat. He's just a regular guy here, but he's been consistent over a long period of time as a devoted follower of Jesus."

The Meek Shall Inherit the Earth

In Colossians 3:12, God's word says His people are to clothe themselves with compassion, kindness, humility, gentleness and patience. As a believer, Pat strives to live with these characteristics. Pat's longtime assistant Andrew Herdliska talked to me about the characteristic that Pat believes stands above the others, saying, "Pat has always said the most attractive quality a person can have is humility. It's something he constantly strives for."

Pat could always be seen standing in the tunnel during Magic home games. He never sat down. Women's basketball head coach at Stetson University Lynn Bria was one who noticed this quirk: "He was always standing behind the bench in the tunnel where the team comes out. He never took a seat." Wondering why, Lynn said, "I asked Pat why he didn't sit down at games. Pat answered, 'That takes someone's seat. They pay for that seat.' I thought it showed how much he cares about his organization because that was someone else's seat, and they need that. It shows his humbleness."

To become a waymaker, you will often stand behind the achievements of others, even though you may have helped guide them on their path to success. Waymakers do not help others for the glory of seeing their names in lights but rather the satisfaction of seeing someone besides themselves be victorious in their own pursuits and passions.

> **Waymakers do not help others for the glory of seeing their names in lights but rather the satisfaction of seeing someone besides themselves be victorious in their own pursuits and passions.**

Pat is constantly able to separate his achievements from others. Andrew talked about how Pat is able to promote in a way that isn't self-aggrandizing, saying, "Pat's into promotion, but not self-promotion." He went on to give an example: "Pat was reading about Twitter in the newspapers before it exploded. And he said, 'We need to do this. It's great promotion.' So we did it, but it's not like we're out there pounding promotions. Instead, he used it to send out motivational quotes and book recommendations because he is an avid reader and people always ask him, 'What should I read?'"

Andrew continued, "He promotes other people's stuff before his own. One time, one of his publishers said, 'That's your competitor's book you're promoting on Twitter.' And Pat's response was 'I don't care.'"

Dwight, Lynn, and Andrew are only a few of the number of people who have noticed Pat's ability to influence and encourage without applause. "I have a master's degree from the University of Florida, but I have a PhD in the Pat Williams School of Leadership," Andrew told me about what the years close to Pat have meant to his life.

Waymakers have the ability to see their lives as an instrument to encourage, advise, or brighten someone else's day. While different from encouragement or advice, brightening someone's day should not be undervalued. In many cases, brightening someone else's day leaves as large an impact as a good piece of timely advice.

Since waymakers aren't able to invest the amount of quality time with every person they come across, a single interaction with a waymaker can not only brighten a day but may still allow a waymaker to, perhaps unintentionally, leave behind a path for others to follow. One such example comes from an interaction Pat had with the Niagara University basketball team in the early 1970s.

The head coach at the time, Frank Layden, said, "We came [to Philadelphia] to play in a tournament around Christmastime, and Pat came out to greet us. One thing I've always known about Pat is that he is very cordial. He was a great host wherever he was, even later on, when I was a coach and he was a general manager in the NBA. When you went to play in his arena, he always made a visit to the locker room before the game. He came and asked if you had everything you needed or 'Is everything orderly?' He wanted everything to be just right. He was running a first-class operation."

The Niagara team players, as well as visiting players from around the NBA, always had a chance to see Pat in action. Pat made himself available and visible, while also making himself scarce and a nonpriority. While some general managers in the league traveled with the teams, Pat had a different philosophy, saying, "The general manager is not meant to be there constantly, monitoring practice, going on the road, or being in the locker room. It's not the place for the GM. Now that doesn't mean he can't be friendly and personable and so forth, but you certainly don't want to get into the coach's way."

After enough encounters with Pat that brightened his day, Frank Layden had built up enough friendship currency with Pat to ask a favor. He said, "We were having a dinner here for a young lady, a police officer's daughter who was hit with a car and was seriously injured. The family needed funds very badly. I called up Pat to come and be our guest speaker. I told him, 'I can't pay you.' He says, 'You don't even have to ask. What time do you want me to be there?' We were in Salt Lake City, and I was giving him about a week's notice, and he came out there on his own dime. He was very generous, never asked for anything and did a great speech. He was very funny, very entertaining. That's the kind of guy I remember and the kind of guy he was."

Humility sometimes prevents Pat from seeing himself as the hero others know him to be. Two great examples of Pat's humility occurred on the floor of the Amway Center—where the Orlando Magic play their home games. The first was another in a long line of stories told to me by Andrew Herdliska. This particular one centered around the Orlando Magic's Hometown Heroes segment—where at each game the Magic recognize someone who works as a first responder or has served in the US military.

One day they asked Pat if he would want to represent the army in an upcoming game because they wanted to honor him for his service. Andrew said Pat was "thrilled beyond belief. He couldn't believe it." And even though Pat has walked on or around the court and been shown on television broadcasts thousands of times during his career, he knew this moment was special. Pat asked Andrew to "please make sure we get that on video."

Andrew told me why he thought that moment was so special to Pat, saying, "Pat's known for a lot of things. He's the basketball guy. The 'adopting kids' guy. The guy who has run all the marathons or wrote all the books. But to be considered one of the Joes in the military, that was different for him."

Pat's oldest daughter, Karyn Williams, shared another story about Pat's humility that was highlighted at center court during an Orlando Magic Hall of Fame induction for her father. Karyn said, "This was a big deal. People were flying in to see my dad be honored. This night was supposed to be all about my dad and what he did for the city of Orlando. Instead, my dad calls his friend Jimmy Hewitt and tells him, 'You were here for the beginning of this, and I want you with me down on the court.'"

Jimmy—who was also cofounder of the Orlando Magic alongside Pat, albeit not as well known—resisted at first, because the night was meant to honor Pat. Karyn, however, remembers hearing her dad tell Jimmy, "Even if nobody in that arena knows who you are or what you did, I know. And it's more important for me to honor you."

I found it interesting when Karyn followed up her story by saying, "Who does that?" I would think most people have an easy time accepting the credit they worked hard for. Waymakers, however, walk in humility and find ways to lift up the names of those around them, like Pat did with Jimmy Hewitt. Since they serve others without the expectation of recognition, waymakers are also able to treasure the unexpected honor that may come from serving, like Pat did when he was called on to be the Hometown Hero. Either way, a waymaker is not motivated by the desire to be seen, yet when a person walks in humility, their life is often seen more clearly. ★

★ ★ ★

CHAPTER EIGHT

MAXIMIZE YOUR TIME

Keep Close to What's Important

The first time I interviewed Pat was for a radio show I hosted in St. Louis called the *New John Simmons Show*. The title was a nickname that reflected my dramatic lifestyle changes after becoming a born-again Christian and subsequent delivery out of a severe gambling addiction.

The goal of the show was to create segments that tried to encourage others how to discover and walk in God's plans and purpose for their lives. In my interview segments, I would invite other Christians who were examples of what living a life following God's plan looked like. Some of my interviews included notable Christian filmmakers, authors, and leaders from ministries and business. The interview I was about to have with Pat was one of the first for my show.

"Hello, is this John?" Pat said as we started what would be the first of many conversations with each other. "It's so nice to talk with you."

My list of preliminary questions centered around Pat's career and involvement in the NBA, but none of those questions were the focus of my interview. Truthfully, I didn't follow the sport of basketball while living in St. Louis, a city that has gone without a professional basketball team for decades. Our town wasn't a hot spot for intrigue and conversation about the game. Instead, I was more excited to talk to Pat about his Christian faith and how it may have propelled him to the heights of success he had achieved.

I introduced Pat to the show with a prewritten list of his lengthy accomplishments and numerous hobbies. I then went off script to share with the listeners how Pat's book *21 Great Leaders* had a profound influence on me. I then thanked Pat for joining me on the show. "Thanks, John. Very nice to talk to you, and thank you for that very, very warm introduction. I appreciate that."

Without hesitation, I decided to ignore my list of introductory questions and instead marched forward excitedly toward the real reason I wanted to bring Pat on the show. "Pat, it's such a pleasure for me to talk with someone who is living out their life in faith by doing things outside the box. A person might think that someone who is living out the life God has for them must have started a ministry or is a pastor of a local church. You are doing more than that, though. And in many different ways"

I followed that thought with my first question: "How do you find the time to do all of the things that you are doing?"

The question was so simple that it almost could've been a throwaway question, had Pat's answer not been so substantial. If Pat had responded in a way that shrugged off the importance of time management or said something like "I just do," I know that you would not be reading this book. Instead, the answer would profoundly impact my personal life and eventually lead me to ask Pat if I could write this book about him.

Pat's answer to my question "How do you find the time to do all of the things that you are doing?" would come in a slow, rhythmic cadence that would be evident in all our conversations: "I keep close to the things that are important to me," followed by a brief pause. Another common trait of his speech pattern.

Pat seems to have a special power where he can briefly search for and quickly find the right words for any question. Pat's slow, methodical answers and pauses reminded me of interviews and programs I had seen of another man of faith I admired—Mr. Rogers.

Pat went on to say, "It's amazing." Another pause. "What you can accomplish in sixteen hours a day, if you stay close to the things that are important to you. Don't do things that are really not leading you anywhere toward your goals in life. I think all of us are capable of accomplishing a lot more than we do."

I thought, "Sixteen hours a day; I had never measured time like that." I immediately began to think of some activities in my life over the years that often made up part of my sixteen hours, like binging television, playing video games, or endlessly scrolling social media apps on my phone. I had asked Pat how he found the time to accomplish so much. I never thought the answer would cause me to question my own use of time in my life. I thought, "How much time am I wasting?" and "What am I capable of that I am not accomplishing?"

Daily Devotion

Our interview moved on from there to questions about his career as an NBA executive and Pat's role as a father to nineteen children and a grandfather to nineteen. We also talked about how he ran four marathons a year, taught Sunday school at church, and hosted his own radio show highlighting authors and their books. I was fascinated to uncover how Pat had grown a life with so many different roots and branches, but throughout our first thirty minutes of conversation together, all I could think about was how he found a way to utilize sixteen hours each day.

I ended my first conversation with Pat by coming back to the idea that he started it with—which was that all people are capable of doing more with their time than they are doing. "Pat, you said there are sixteen hours in a day. What might you encourage people to find time for in their lives to find success?"

"Well," Pat said before a final pause, "you've got to spend time with God every day. It's so important to spend time with God, reading the Bible and in quiet time of prayer. Spend time talking to the Lord. He wants to hear from you. You get the privilege of talking to Him and then quietly waiting. He will respond to you.

"Plus," Pat went on to add, "find a good Bible-teaching church where you can spend your time on the weekend gathering together with other believers. That's a big part of life."

Time management is an important lesson for waymakers to learn, because time is the most valuable resource we have. Time is valuable because it is the only resource we can't get back once we use it. Time is also one of the only resources that is not for sale. Pat has made sure his days include a daily routine of exercises of faith, including Bible reading and prayer.

Pat's viewpoint on managing time effectively was a key to opening the door to many successes in his life. Pat understood the need to treasure and manage his time with great care. His ability to maintain closeness to the things he cared about also consistently allowed him to reach goals throughout his life. For you and me, the more goals we check off our list, the more time we can devote to finding new paths.

No Ordinary Paper

One of the efforts Pat has devoted a lot of time to is his daily newspaper reading. "Every day of my life starts with five newspapers in the driveway," Pat said about his daily habit. He went on to say, "Before anything happens in my day, I gather those papers and read them. I read every section and every page. I live for newspapers. I can't function in any day without them.

"I learned to read, really, by reading the *New York Times* sports section when I was seven because I'd become so interested in baseball," Pat said before sharing what papers make up his daily collection. "I read the *Orlando Sentinel, USA Today, Wall Street Journal, New York Post*, and *New York Times*. We've got 'lefty' papers there, and we got 'righties.' We have a nice little balance."

Writer Michael Mink is a contributor to the paper *Investor's Business Daily*. Michael—who also worked on a couple of book projects with Pat—knew when Pat had read the current issue. He said, "Pat would always call me after I did an article. If we didn't talk, he'd leave a message and talk about what was positive about the article." This type of behavior is also part of Pat's friendship currency that we will discuss in a future chapter.

In addition to reading the news, Pat is also gathering it for distribution. As he reads an article, he will rip out those that interest him or help someone he knows. The origin of this practice is unknown, but Pat's kids remember their dad tearing off articles of their particular interest or a note of encouragement and taping it to the door of their bedroom for them to read later. The kids did not get a reprieve once they left the house either. Pat's son Bobby said, "He's been sending me stuff since I've been in college."

Sending newspaper clippings is a big part of Pat's life now. He enjoys tearing out articles and thinking about what the person receiving them might feel or think about the contents. Some of the clippings are sent off to his typist for inclusion in his index card system. Others are handed out at work.

For Pat's assistant Andrew Herdliska, the practice of sending out Pat's clippings to other people became a routine part of his job. He said, "We ended up buying something from Office Depot that was like a mini mailroom. It had sixteen or twenty slots. We labeled all the people he likes to send his clippings to, and we would do a systematic mailing every week or two."

While spending so much time reading multiple papers and saving the clippings may not seem like an exercise in maximizing time, Pat is able to multitask various projects with this one activity. He stays current on today's news, collects stories for his books, and thinks about his friends and family. Each time Pat sends a clipping off to someone, he is actually honoring them, because he is showing them love and attention. This act cultivates the ground of his many friendships and does not go unnoticed.

One of Pat's friendships was with the MLB's 1948 Rookie of the Year Alvin Dark. Over the years, Pat would often visit Alvin and his wife, Jackie, at their home and discuss baseball or their shared love for Christ. After Alvin passed away in 2014, Pat continued to keep Jackie lifted up. She said, "Pat sends different things to me that he sees to let me know they're still talking about my husband. It's so sweet."

From the spouse of a former baseball player to megachurch pastor and *Turning Point* host Dr. David Jeremiah, Pat's clippings are reaching and personal. Dr. Jeremiah shared, "One time I had a book that made it to the top of the bestsellers list. Pat was flying across the country, saw it in *USA Today*, and ripped it out and sent it to me. He said, 'Hey, you made it to the big time, kid.' That's just what he does. That's the kind of person he is."

The constant attention Pat shows each relationship in his life lends to their longevity and helps add to the great respect and love so many have for Pat. Pat's generosity doesn't stop at newspaper clippings, however. Dr. Jeremiah added, "Many years ago, he invited me to do a chapel for the Phillies. I did the chapel, and we talked a lot and got to be friends. Since then, I've done a lot of stuff for the NBA. I've done probably two or three all-star chapels for them over the years, and whenever I go to Orlando, I always call him. He gets me seats on the floor for the Magic. He actually just did a beautiful endorsement for a book that I have coming out in the fall. He's always ready to help. He does anything he can to encourage you." ★

CHAPTER NINE

MANEUVER OVER OBSTACLES

Facing Opposition for the First Time

"In 1966, my second year in Spartanburg, the Phillies provided us with a terrific crop of young players. We won the championship going away. We set attendance records. It was an absolute Cinderella season," Pat said soon after declaring this story was the one do-over in life he would take if he could. "At the end of the season, the Phillies wanted me to come up and meet with them in Philadelphia. They wanted me to move from Spartanburg and become the general manager for their new AA franchise in Reading, Pennsylvania."

Pat continued, "I went up there as this super promoter and executive after a marvelous season, but what I did up there still embarrasses me. I basically said, 'Reading isn't going to work. It's not a good baseball city.' I said things that were awful, mainly because I was scared. After about an hour, they'd had enough. They got up and left.

I was sitting there thinking, 'What have I done?'"

While Pat later spent more than a decade as a GM of the 76ers in the city of Philadelphia, after that meeting he realized his boyhood dream to manage the Phillies inside Connie Mack Stadium was gone. "I fouled the nest," Pat said. "My upward mobility in the Phillies organization was over."

A blowdown, or deadfall, is a hiking term used to describe a tree or shrub that has fallen across the trail. When facing a blowdown, a hiker is forced to maneuver over, under, or around the obstacle to continue along his or her path. Similarly, the path of a waymaker will face blowdowns in life that force them to stop and deal with an obstacle prior to moving further ahead. These moments, however, will often lead us to a place where we will be in prime position to help others who will later navigate a similar obstacle.

Pat headed back to Spartanburg to general manage the 1967 season. He also took time to make apology calls to the Phillies organization. While Pat was unsure about his future at the time, he looks back now and sees how that obstacle became an opportunity. He said, "We were getting ready for the 1968 season. It was in February of that year that I was introduced to Jesus Christ. I made a decision to receive Him and accept Him into my life. I turned my life over to Him, and that changed the entire course of my life.

"Had I gone to Reading, that may have never happened," Pat continued. "I might have never met the Lord. It's funny how God uses our humbling experiences, our failures, and our poor decisions. Even in the midst of my arrogance and horrible display in front of the Phillies brass in September of 1966. He can still utilize us, even though we're not aware of Him."

Not every obstacle we face in life has a clear path for us to take in order to get around it. On a person's journey to become a waymaker, deciding to face the obstacle instead of turning back is sometimes as important as figuring out how to maneuver past it. Pat faced his obstacle by apologizing and doing what he could to smooth things over, but he also believed he had damaged the potential of his future.

While Pat felt his opportunities with the Phillies were limited, he was only beginning on the path God had for him. A few months after finding Christ in his 1968 season, Jack Ramsey called with an offer for Pat to work in pro basketball—where Pat spent the next fifty years of his career. Making choices without God is what led Pat to making a mistake in that meeting to begin with. Pat said, "I was not in Philadelphia thinking, 'Lord, please protect my lips.' I wouldn't have had any idea about that." Pat's blowdown was only overcome through his newly formed relationship and reliance on Christ to guide his path.

Turning Obstacles into Opportunities

Pat currently has a vision to launch the Orlando Dreamers MLB team sometime in the next decade. In undertaking that project, however, Pat knows that his vision many not come to pass. As successful as Pat's vision to bring pro basketball to Orlando was, not every vision he has had since has been as fruitful as the Magic. Two failed attempts to bring pro baseball to Orlando and a lost Women's National Basketball Association (WNBA) team have preceded Pat's current adventure. Regarding adversity, chasing a vision that goes unfulfilled can produce valuable lessons—while also instilling hope that the vision may still come to pass later in life.

Pat recounted the days of baseball expansion efforts past, saying, "The first was in '90–'91. The second was in the mid-'90s. They expanded the first time in Miami. The second time, they expanded into St. Petersburg but called the team Tampa Bay. We tried twice and lost out to the bigger markets."

In many ways, going through the logistics of launching an expansion team today is similar to what Pat and his teams did in the '90s. There are, however, some stark differences. Pat said, "The price of expansion was $95 million. Today, it would be well over $1 billion. The cost of the ballparks back then would be around $60 million. Today, it's like $1.2 billion. It was a far different world."

Pat continued to share about those first two attempts to bring baseball to Orlando, saying, "We went through the whole procedure. We got people to make commitments on season tickets in advance. We had renderings for the ballpark. We had the location; it was in the city. We had a strong owner. We did everything we could." Pat later asked those who made the decisions on expansions why Orlando wasn't selected. They said, "We took helicopter rides over Miami and Orlando. When we went over to Miami, all we saw were house tops. When we went over Orlando, all we saw were tree tops."

While the perceived lack of population was partly to blame for Orlando not being chosen, the efforts did bring Pat together with possibly his greatest waymaker relationship—the DeVos family. "The DeVos family could've planted roots and gotten involved in any city in America besides their home in Grand Rapids. While they have ever been faithful to that city, they chose Orlando, Florida, as their second city," Pat said before describing his introduction to Amway owner Rich DeVos.

"Do we trust Pat and sign up for this adventure? The answer was yes."

"I had gone up there and invited Rich to become the owner of the expansion baseball team. I had never met him, and I did not know him. I didn't have anything other than a little sheet of paper. Today, that would be done with video and overhead lighting. Then, it was just me with a notepad and my pitch."

Pat continued, "I was ushered into his room to give him my baseball pitch, and Rich listened. Then they excused me. [T]hey ushered me back in, and he said, 'Tell the National League I will go forward with them.'" Rich DeVos's son, Dick DeVos, said that even though the baseball expansion effort "ultimately failed, the Magic opportunity emerged."

Dick DeVos added, "As a family, we had always thought that being involved in professional sports would be fascinating, interesting, and potentially a terrific platform to reach young people and be an encouragement to the community." The question, Dick then said, was "Do we trust Pat and sign up for this adventure? The answer was yes."

The original ownership group was local to Orlando. Pat said, "Bill DuPont was the principal owner. They owned the team for the first two years and then felt it was time to sell." The timing of Pat's newfound relationship with Rich seemed kismet. Pat said, "The DeVos family was [in Orlando] because of baseball. They liked it here. They felt very welcome. They decided as a family to buy the Magic. They've owned it now for thirty years."

Bill Boer was the chief operating officer (COO) of the RDV Corporation—which oversaw the DeVos family finances—and was closely connected to Pat during the ownership transition of the Magic. Bill said, "I think it was Pat's integrity that really helped convince the DeVos family. We worked together on different projects. For example, building their headquarters. It's called the RDV Sportsplex. It's where their home offices are, and the team practices there."

Bill's father-in-law also happened to be Sam Bell—who was once the head track coach at Pat's second alma mater, Indiana University. That connection to Pat inducted Bill as a member of Pat's newspaper-clipping club. He said, "Pat would get articles about my father-in-law and send them to me." He added, "About a week after my father-in-law died, there was an article in the *New York Times* about him. Pat called me out of the blue to express his sympathy. He's that kind of person. A loyal, great guy."

That positive first impression Pat had on Rich DeVos has since had long-lasting ramifications, not only for them both as individuals, but the community of Orlando as a whole. After Rich DeVos—who passed away in 2018—and his family bought the Magic in 1991 for $85 million, they became prominent fixtures during the rise and growth of Orlando that has continued to blossom more every year.

As part of the sale, Pat—who was a 1 percent owner of the Magic as founder—was bought out by the DeVos family. Pat said, "It turned out to be about $1 million. I had never seen that kind of money before. Never dreamed about it. In those days, it was a scary amount of money because the big salaries that sports executives have today had not yet arrived." He shared the waymaker luxury that million-dollar check provided by saying, "With that money, we were able to see that all our kids' college education was taken care of."

In the years that followed their purchase of the Magic, the DeVos family impacted the city of Orlando through business development and philanthropic ventures. In addition to the Magic, the DeVos family brought in the Orlando Solar Bears minor-league hockey team and WNBA Orlando Miracle—which have since left Orlando and are now the Connecticut Sun. The ultimate positive impact the DeVos family has had on Orlando is immeasurable; however, it was Pat's vision and ability to build friendships that brought them here to begin with. Pat making a way for the DeVos family to plant roots in Orlando not only changed the course of their family's life but also made a way for the entire community of Orlando to be impacted by their arrival in some way.

Dick talked about how Pat was able to connect his family with the people of Orlando, saying, "Pat has the ability to tell a story. His ability helps people capture a vision and a future that he saw of how Orlando could move into and become a first-tier community with a top-level sports team in it. The support the Magic enjoyed when we showed up on the scene was, I think, a tribute to Pat and to his energy.

"The Magic is kind of the Disney World for the people who live in Orlando," Dick continued. "Everybody thinks that Disney World defines Orlando, but I think for the people who live in Orlando, the Magic have provided some definition to Orlando and have created the social center, if you will, for those who live in the Orlando community. They come together at the games and watch them. There is interaction and camaraderie amongst the folks from Orlando leadership, folks who live there and are just trying to raise a family—who are working there every day, all across the economic and social spectrum. The Magic was the place where Orlando came together."

Tough Losses

In 1962, the Wake Forest Demon Deacons baseball team was playing an NCAA regional tournament where the winner would advance to the College World Series—held annually in Omaha, Nebraska. Pat missed his graduation in order to play in the tournament. Pat said, "All we needed was one win on the last day. It was double elimination. Florida State won both games. The last one was an eleven-inning heartbreaker in the rain.

"He must have thrown 250 pitches," Pat said about his battery mate Don "Goose" Roth, who pitched every inning of that game. "We had no more pitchers. We lost in the eleventh inning. It's still among the three most painful losses in my sports career. It never goes away."

Pat added, "My dad was there for the game. Afterward, we said goodbye. He headed up with my sister, Carol, dropped her off in Washington but never made it home to Wilmington."

"A few of us from the team stopped in Richmond to see a minor-league game," Don Roth said about traveling north back home after the tournament. He added, "All of the state police were out looking for us to alert Pat, but nobody could find us." Pat said, "In those days, there was no way to reach people. Eventually, I got home and found out my dad had died in a car wreck."

Pat's cousin Robin Williams recalled traveling to the game in the car with his uncle James Williams but left with other family afterward. He said, "I rode with Jim across the state to watch Pat play those two games. The second game was a devastating loss for Pat. I was standing by Uncle Jim when we went down in the dugout, and Jim consoled him. Pat was distraught; he didn't say much in return. Then everyone left. Jim dropped Pat's sister Carol off where she was living and fell asleep on his way home, ran into an abutment, and died."

Bill Covington played second base for Pat's Wake Forest team and spoke of James Williams death, saying, "Pat's father would come to see us play and then take us out to dinner. His nickname was Gentleman Jim, and he was one of the finest men I've ever met. It was just a tragic thing that happened."

After attending the funeral, new college graduate Pat's thoughts turned quickly back to baseball and how it would play a role in his future because of the last conversation he had with his father. Pat said, "I had asked my dad after that game if he would talk to Mr. Carpenter for me. He said, 'Why don't you wait until you get home.'" Indirectly, that conversation and the bond between Pat's dad, James, and his good friend and Phillies club owner Bob Carpenter led to the meeting where Pat got into professional baseball, which we discussed earlier in chapter 1.

"My dad was extremely excited about being in my life," Pat said as he discussed both the encouraging role he played in Pat's life while he was alive and the void that was left after he was gone. "He relished seeing me have success as a college athlete. When I was younger, his exuberance embarrassed me, but he was my fan. He would've definitely enjoyed all of my career.

"He was fifty-five when he died. If he had lived another thirty years, I would have been fifty-two, and he would have seen me through my first year in Philadelphia, my years in Chicago, my year in Atlanta. He would've seen all twelve years back in Philadelphia, including the championship and the parade. He would have seen my first six years of the Magic. He would've met all nineteen children and been wild about them."

Pat concluded his thought by saying, "But the accident happened. We were all shocked. We still haven't found out what happened. All we can do is guess, but we gave that up long ago."

Tragedy in the form of a death in the family struck Pat's family again years later when one of his adopted children—Richard, whom the family called Richie—was killed in a shooting in 2017. Like with his father, Pat said, "We never really found out what happened." Both of these moments have created waves of heartache in his life.

Pat, however, has stayed optimistic even after facing obstacles, saying, "I'm now in a position to help someone who has lost their dad at a young age." Always turning adversity on its side, Pat looks to focus on the good that can come out of a difficult situation instead of dwelling on the hurt and pain. Not always easy to do, but something he learned to do consistently whenever adversity would blow down in front of his path.

The Big Three

Adversity comes in multiple sizes, while lessons and faith can be tested in each blowdown we come across. Pat's "big three" events, as he calls them, are the ones where he has been tested in such a way that others could benefit from following him through similar paths in their own lives.

"The first one was in 1947, when the fourth child was born into our family," Pat said to begin a long conversation that included honest retellings of his greatest moments of sufferings. "In those days, children could not go up and see the mother. All you can do is stand out in the parking lot and wave up to the window. You didn't know in advance in those days what the baby was going to be. It was a girl. My third sister. Oh, I was upset; I wanted a brother."

Later, Pat said, "We noticed Mary Ellen was not advancing well. We did not really understand that. The doctors didn't. Eventually my parents came to grips with the fact that they had what was then known as a mentally retarded child. Today, you would call them [children with] Down syndrome. That was the first real heartache at our family."

Mary Ellen—who lived into her forties—spent her life being cared for in a facility run by the state of Delaware, but Pat said, "We would go down to see her. Not regularly. My mother went down every month. It was about a two-hour drive. She went down every month to see Mary Ellen faithfully. Our parents felt that to have her at home would have made the other three of us have a much more difficult childhood and we would have had less parental time because Mary Ellen would need constant care. Not every family would have done that, but in our case, I think it was the right decision.

"The next big crisis was Jill walking away and leaving our marriage. I came home one day and she was gone. I was mortified, embarrassed," Pat said. "We had written books, spoken at churches, and been huge advocates of strong marriages. I had gone through some tough times with her, trying to be the husband that she wanted, and I never was successful in doing that."

Pat added, "We were running our own boarding house. As it turns out, it was too much for her. She was overwhelmed. She didn't see a way out. In the spring of 1994, she just left. No note. Nothing. She never returned—which ultimately led to our divorce a year later."

Shocked at what had happened, Pat turned to God in the midst of his trouble and confusion. He said, "I learned that God is still good through it all, because I had peace in my heart when I realized that we don't have control over other people. They are free to make their own decisions. That's how God made us."

Even filled with God's peace, Pat said, "It was a huge shock when she just left. Particularly when I ended up single-parenting eighteen children for about three years." Providing for his family became a focused priority in Pat's life. He said, "My family had an $80,000-a-year food bill. You'd better be producing some revenue to pay for that. So I was helping to run an NBA basketball team, speaking, and writing to try and pay all the bills." He added, "Fortunately, we had help."

One of the people who stepped up to help the Williams family in a big way during that season of their lives was Macario Garcia—whom everyone calls Angel—a fitting nickname for the role he served in the Williams family. "I was a carpenter at his house when he first came down here to Florida. He bought a house on Lee Road in 1988," said Angel—who later transitioned from a rarely used carpenter to a handyman.

Angel remembers Pat's daily routine: "He would wake up at five in the morning to exercise and take the kids to school. Then he would come home, run five miles, and eat breakfast. Then he went to a full day's work, and he'd come home about eight o'clock at night. He was a hard worker.

"Later on," Angel continued, "as he adopted more kids, Pat would always have time for everybody. If I had a problem or the kids had a problem, he was there for everybody. He would also read his newspapers every day, and he would take little sections out of them and go to the kid's door and pin them on the door so the kids know what's going on in life."

After the divorce, Angel said Pat was "strained," and Pat approached him one day while he was cutting the grass, saying, "Angel, I need help." Angel replied, "From me? What can I do?" Pat said, "I need you to help me raise these kids." Angel soon found his role around the house transitioning once again, saying, "I started taking them to school and picking them up and taking them to sports. With eighteen kids, we were always on the road."

Waymakers can often be seen as the person other people call on in times of trouble. Waymakers, however, are not immune to needing help themselves. Pat said Angel "was there doing a multitude of tasks. So I did have help, but I was still traveling, still speaking." Realizing the adversity Pat was facing, Angel was quick to help when Pat's schedule took him away from home, saying, "Sometimes, Pat had to leave, or he'd come in late at night. Sometimes he was gone for two or three days. I was always there for the kids. I would sit there with them. They would cry on my shoulder or tell me their problems."

Not only did Pat offer Angel waymaker opportunities in the form of work, but he allowed him to make a way into his growing family and help care for the most precious part of his life—his children. Angel never expected to be so close to the family when he showed up to add an addition to their home decades ago. Today, however, he realizes how special the opportunity he was given was.

He said, "When [Pat's son] Alan graduated, he said, 'Dad's out there in the audience, and I want to thank him so much for bringing me from Brazil and giving me a life here in America. And then I want to thank my second dad, Angel, for taking care of me and keeping me out of trouble.'"

Don't Waste Your Sufferings

"The other big issue was the cancer diagnosis," Pat said about his most recent battle with adversity. Diagnosed with multiple myeloma in January 2011, Pat spoke up about his journey with cancer in his book *The Mission Is Remission*. Currently the mission is successful, as Pat has been in remission for several years. The initial diagnosis, however, shocked Pat, and his inquisitive nature began to lead to many questions for his doctor.

Pat asked, "What's multiple myeloma? What does *multiple* mean? Why did this happen? How did this happen? Why me? What did I do wrong? What's the life expectancy? What do we do? How do we tell our children? What do I do about work? What do we say to the public?

"Fortunately," Pat said, "My wife, Ruth, was there to take notes on all of this and write down the answers to all of our questions. Dr. Robert Reynolds was so helpful in guiding us through that moment. We told our children and then had a press conference to tell the public what was going on."

When the news finally settled, Pat said, "I was faced with one of two decisions: either shake my fist angrily in the face of God or dive into His lap and hold Him so tightly that you couldn't see any space

> "I was faced with one of two decisions: either shake my fist angrily in the face of God or dive into His lap and hold Him so tightly that you couldn't see any space between us. I elected to do the latter."

between us. I elected to do the latter."

Founder of the Multiple Myeloma Research Foundation Kathy Giusti was a valuable part of helping Pat walk through his journey. Kathy said, "I helped him to understand critical decisions that he would have to make to optimize his outcomes. One of those early decisions was to make sure that he had a strong team experienced in treating multiple myeloma. We were in close touch as he went through his stem cell transplant, which is a standard treatment for multiple myeloma but which also can be very toxic for patients.

"Like most cancer patients," Kathy added, "Pat did not know what to expect from either the disease or the treatments, nor did he know how to successfully navigate the complicated healthcare system. From the time I met him, however, Pat has shown extraordinary courage, strength, and positivity. He has inspired countless patients and many others in the multiple myeloma community by speaking openly and publicly about his diagnosis and challenges he faced adjusting to his new normal."

Peter Kerasotis covered Pat's cancer battle for *Orlando Magazine*. He noticed how Pat needed to shift from motivator to overcomer, saying, "It's one thing to write a book about success, positive thinking, and leadership, but what's going to happen when you need to start applying those principles and maxims from all of those sayings and anecdotes that you've accumulated and apply it to yourself now in this cancer battle?

"I went to a clinic and sat with him during one of his chemo treatments," Peter said. "Pat told me, 'I had to get out of myself and what was going on with me and turn into the guy that is encouraging all the other people battling cancer.'"

Pat's vulnerability to speak up about the valleys of his life, including his cancer diagnosis, unfulfilled visions, or his divorce are also what make him an effective communicator. These incidents aren't stains on a great life; they are examples of how a waymaker maneuvers over obstacles and adversity. Pat's desire to use his experiences and lessons from hardship is clearly the trait of a waymaker.

Pat concluded his thoughts about the lasting effect these "big three" events had on his life, saying, "In every case, the words of my pastor in Chicago, Warren Wiersbe, ring true: 'Pat, don't waste your sufferings.' That is probably the best piece of advice I've ever gotten, because in those tough times, we're very teachable. In those tough times, we are very open to the Lord's teachings. We're sensitive. We are not full of ourselves, because we've been leveled.

"What Dr. Wiersbe meant was at the end of this suffering period—and it's not going to last forever—you want to be sharper, more knowledgeable, and more sensitive. You want to have a better heart for people's needs. If you haven't gotten that through the suffering, well, then you've wasted the suffering.

"In every case, they are certainly not what I would have wanted, but I'm also convinced that God allows those things, and He expects us to learn and grow from them. Eventually, He is going to bring triumph out of the tragedy," Pat said before summing up the lessons and impact his sufferings have had on the lives of others.

"I'm in a position now to talk to any family that has a Down syndrome child. I'm in a position now to talk to anybody who loses their dad at a young age. I'm in a position now, as I have over the years, to help any man whose wife has left him. I certainly did not plan to have a cancer diagnosis, but as a result, I have been on the receiving end of countless requests to talk to someone who has just been diagnosed, who is terrified, worried, nervous, and scared. I certainly didn't volunteer, but as a result, God has called me into the cancer counseling business. I didn't see that one coming."

Counseling Business

During the course of writing this book, I saw in person one of those opportunities for Pat to use his own sufferings to help others come up. When I spoke with best-selling sports author Rich Wolfe, I learned he was recently diagnosed with life-threating cancer himself. Rich asked if I could get him in contact with Pat because he knew it could be an encouragement. Rich said, "Pat does not know I am sick, and it would be great to talk with him. I don't know if I've ever met a finer person." When I gave Pat the news, he hung up with me to call Rich—his waymaking instincts kicked in without a second's notice.

The opportunity with Rich was only one in a myriad of stories where Pat used his experience facing blowdowns to lead others behind him through similar terrain. Upon his entrance into professional sports as an executive, Ron Dick said, "I got three thanks but no thanks from the Phillies, the Eagles, and the Flyers before the Sixers, and Pat Williams took a chance on me."

After Pat acted as a waymaker for Ron's early career, Ron describes himself now as "a practitioner who became an academic" because of his more recent role as associate professor of sports marketing at Duquesne University. A few years ago, Ron also said Pat "helped mentor me through colon cancer, which I had removed in just nine days, which was great."

A month prior to Pat's eightieth birthday in May of 2020, Orlando Magic owner Dick DeVos shared the story of the sister-in-law of his close friend who had been diagnosed with multiple myeloma. Dick said, "I happened to be on a conference call and [my friend] was sharing how devastated she was with the news. It immediately came to me. I said, 'Well, she needs to talk to Pat because Pat will be able to be an encouragement to her in a way that none of us can.' So I reached out to Pat, and within two days Pat had made the connection, been in touch, and talked to her."

Dick continued, "They cried together and laughed together on the phone. Pat sent her a copy of his book, and I presume they've been in touch ever since. So even as he approached his eightieth birthday, he was immediately happy to go out, make the call, make the contact, and try to be an encouragement to this woman who was struggling with a really difficult diagnosis. 'How can I help?' That's Pat's attitude."

Another example of Pat using his sufferings to encourage others came from author and Pat's fellow speaker on the circuit Don Yaeger. Don said, "I'll never forget a few years back, Pat was in Tallahassee, and he had let me know he was here. I said, 'Hey, we've actually got some clients from a company that I own who are going to be over at our home. My wife is cooking dinner tonight. Would you have any interest in joining us?' I knew Pat was going through his cancer treatment. So I knew the steroids were affecting him, and I knew he was probably uncomfortable with the puffiness around his face and a little bit around his body and other things."

After Pat accepted the invitation to dinner, however, Don said, "You could not tell that the man was fighting cancer because he was just so upbeat. The group of folks that I had over were mesmerized by Pat. No one could tell how bad his condition was."

Recently retired Rolf Zettersten was senior vice president at Hachette Book Group and published several of Pat's titles. Rolf has noticed that Pat will not let sickness slow him down. He said, "Pat's enthusiasm is infectious, and it rubs off on you. He has a lot of creativity and energy. In terms of productivity, there are very few authors I know that can generate as much material as Pat does. It's just phenomenal. In recent years, he was struggling with illness and still managed to keep pushing forward. I have great admiration for him."

Wake Forest athletic director Ron Wellman spoke to both Pat's courage and stubbornness to keep going even while sick, saying, "He came to Winston-Salem to give a speech. I introduced him, and I have never seen a man so sick give a speech. He sat on a chair, and he literally had a nose bleed the entire time he was speaking. He went through all kinds of hankies. I encouraged him to stop. He wouldn't hear of that at all, and he gave one of the best speeches you'd ever heard.

"The next week," Ron said, "he called me from the hospital. I think he had pneumonia or some really severe medical situation, but he would not bow out of his commitment. That is just who Pat Williams is. I remember when he had cancer and he was in the hospital. I talked with him a couple of times, and he'd tell me how many laps he took around the floor. He was counting them, and I'll never forget his comment. He said, 'Ron, I'm breaking all kinds of records. No one has ever done this many laps on the second day after surgery.'"

While Pat will often try to stay positive and make the best of his situations, walking through adversity isn't always easy. Bobby Pinson, who is the son-in-law of Pat's former boss and first spiritual father R. E. Littlejohn, has known Pat for fifty-five years and has been witness to many of Pat's battles. "We've been close to Pat all these years. When he would travel through Spartanburg, he would often stop and spend the night with us," Bobby said about how they have stayed connected over the years.

Bobby remembers one night in particular when Pat shared his vulnerability, saying, "He was going through that divorce. He came up here, and he was telling my wife, Dixie, and me all about what took place. I had a real nice comfortable chair, and he was kind of leaned back. I think he was comfortable, and he just got to talking.

That was a very interesting experience because Pat was always so confident and so much in charge. You never thought that would have happened to him."

Terry Pluto is a sportswriter who met Pat while covering the NBA beat in 1985. Terry has deduced why Pat has both the ability to pass over his own down moments as well as lead others over their own, saying, "The really nice thing about Pat, along with the incredible story of all those kids he adopted, is that he has a really positive attitude. The way he's come through [multiple myeloma]; he had the divorce and job changes. I like the bounce-back part of Pat Williams. His ability to go from 'why me' to 'what's next' has really helped him.

"It's something I learned from people like him. Certainly, they have their moments staring at the ceiling and wondering what's going on, but come morning they're on to the next thing. That's what I really picked up from Pat—the resiliency. It's always easy to talk about somebody else's resiliency, but it's really hard to apply it to yourself." ★

CHAPTER TEN

READ A BOOK

Leaders are Readers

Harry Truman has been quoted as saying, "Not all readers are leaders, but all leaders must be readers." This quote certainly applies to waymakers as well. Over the years, Pat has been able to make leadership look effortless; however, his ability to lead others, which is the defining characteristic of a waymaker, has been a lifelong position for Pat.

Waymakers are lifelong learners. And reading, like listening to your mentor for things unknown, is another method of capturing new information. Reading is arguably the easiest way to learn from the experiences of others, and waymakers know the value in learning those lessons. Leadership follows throughout the lives of readers because they are then able to take the lessons they learned from reading and put their cumulative knowledge into practice.

If all leaders are readers, then it would seem Pat's leadership skills and subsequent successes can be attributed to the extreme effort it has taken him to read an extraordinary number of books. For Pat, his foray into reading began at the age of seven while turning the pages of the *New York Times* on the floor of his childhood home in Delaware. "I would study the box scores. My family soon realized that if they gave me baseball books, I would read them. I did. I saved them too. I still have them," Pat said about his early glimpse into the world of reading.

"Reading is the greatest exercise you can do for your cranial muscle—which needs exercise every day," Pat said about his favorite hobby. According to Pat's sister Ruth Cornelison, that habit took time to develop. She said, "My sister and I were pretty smart. We were English majors. So was our mom. Pat just stuck out like a sore thumb in terms of academics. He just couldn't care less during his years playing sports in high school and college.

"I would help him do his homework. I would help him read his books. It was a struggle for Pat to even get through whatever he was assigned to read, and we had heavy-duty homework in this private school that we went to. The only reason we were in this private school, Tower Hill, was because our dad was a teacher there initially. We got a big deal on our tuition. But my mom and my dad would be coaching him because we had to read books and write papers.

"Oh, it makes my blood run cold," Ruth said about the workload given to the Williams children during their time at Tower Hill. "So Pat needed a lot of help, and I think he willingly took it. That's why it's so astounding to me, how he rocketed away and out of sight from his early days of academia."

By learning to exercise his brain, Pat has now reached a new level of reading, learning, and comprehension. His sister certainly notices how far Pat has come. She said, "He runs circles around us with all his reading and his interest in books and his writing books and so forth. It's spectacular." Ruth added, "We had a very severe English teacher at Tower Hill named Herb Oviatt. He was tough."

Pat, too, remembers that Mr. Oviatt "was a little guy, but he was relentless. He wouldn't settle for anything but the best. He was a stickler for good vocabulary. That's what most people would remember about him. To this day, I have a dictionary next to my reading chair because words pop up as you're reading. What does that mean? And usually you can just blow by it and forget it. But I'm finding more and more, I want to know what the word means. And that is in honor of Mr. Oviatt." Ruth says Pat continually says to her, "I wonder if Herb is listening? I hope he's paying attention to what I finally did."

Either way, Pat's time at Tower Hill has left quite an indelible impression. Current head of school at Tower Hill Bessie Spears said, "We are proud to call Pat a Tower Hill alum and have enjoyed having him back on campus to speak to students about leadership and his career path. He is a motivational speaker and understands how to relate to students, teams, athletes, and inspire the best in human nature."

Maximizing Time

Some would say that Pat is an avid reader. The term *avid* implies that Pat has an interest in reading. Pat's love for books goes far beyond that term, however, because Pat is obsessive in his desire to read. On average, Pat finishes reading one book a day, although he is usually reading five or six books at the same time, spread out between the locations he frequents. His favorite books are historical biographies.

In his free time, Pat hardly ever watches television. Instead, he fills his time reading a book. Most people like to read a little at night, on a rainy day, or maybe on the airplane. Pat has taken the notion of "finding a time to read" to new heights.

Considering the sheer volume of material Pat reads each year, finding unique places and times to read has become normal for Pat. The most notable of those unique places, of course, is the tunnel during Magic games. Friend Charlie Morgan, who would sometimes stand next to Pat in the tunnel during games, said that reading wasn't the only activity Pat found time for. Charlie said during the first time-out of the game, "Pat took off. I turned around, and he was running. He ran into the fitness room, jumped on the bike, and started peddling like mad at the highest speed."

Charlie continued, "There was a TV set right there. So he's watching the game, and as soon as it says, 'All right, now back to play,' he jumped off the bike and came running back to the tunnel. He did that in every single time-out. And I thought, 'Man, this guy has got more energy. He is just amazing. I just can't keep up with him.'"

Besides the tunnel, accounts of Pat reading in unique places and times came from many sources. Assistant Andrew Herdliska remembers being surprised after learning about one of Pat's reading spots, saying, "He would take a book in the car with him and at stoplights would start reading the book." When Andrew talked to Pat about the safety of reading while driving, Pat said, "I'm just sitting here at a stoplight. I might as well knock out two pages."

Another way Pat uses his time to combine his passions for reading and communication is on his radio show, *Pat Williams Weekend Hour*. On the show, Pat interviews nonfiction authors of all types and discusses their books while an Orlando audience listens in.

Show engineer Chris Crawford expounded on Pat's uniqueness as an interviewer, saying, "He doesn't ask specific questions about the book. He goes chapter by chapter and asks the author to explain what he or she meant. When I first started working for his show, I thought this was a weird way to interview someone, but every single author loves the way he does it. Afterwards, they will say, 'This has been my favorite way to conduct an interview about my book. I'm going to tell my publicist to get more people to do that with me.' Pat establishes little relationships with them this way, and they love to come back."

While not specific to Pat's obsession with reading, NBA coach Bob Hill has also seen Pat multitask to maximize time in unique ways. First, he said, "He had a radio show he invited me to, and he ate a swordfish dinner while we were live on the radio. I mean, he's the only person in Orlando, maybe in America, that could get away with something like that, because you just love the guy."

Another moment occurred during road trips. Bob said, "He used to carry weights with him in his suitcase. They were the kind of weights where you fill them up with water, so they didn't weigh anything when he put them in the suitcase. Then he'd get in his room, and he'd be lifting weights, trying to maintain some sense of strength." Similarly, Andrew shared that he also saw Pat exercise in unique places, including while making copies. "He would lean into the countertop and start banging out push-ups, and Pat was like, 'I'm going to be standing here for thirty seconds. I might as well do some push-ups.'"

Pat loves to find ways to maximize his time. Book reading and physical fitness are just two examples of this methodology that are often on display wherever he goes. During a trip together to New York for a taping of *Fox and Friends*, daughter Karyn stayed in a hotel room with her father. At the end of the evening, Pat sat at the side table to read his daily-bread devotional as Karyn got ready for bed. She remembers seeing her dad read every night, but it had been years since they stayed together. She shared that her dad's focus on reading didn't stop simply because he was on the road or because he had gotten older, saying, "He's so methodical. He's so disciplined about all his little things. He does not miss a day of somehow trying to pour something into his heart or glean something else from another writer."

A focus on maximizing time is how Pat reads five hundred books a year, which he has done for decades. After keeping every book he has ever read as a trophy, his collection of books numbers over thirty thousand titles. Those titles will soon be put on the shelves of the Pat Williams Leadership Library inside his home church, First Baptist Orlando.

> **Focus is an indicative trait of a waymaker. Waymakers, however, maintain focus on things that are equally as important to them as they are self-improving.**

The same time-maximizing focus that allows Pat to read so many book titles is also the focus that allowed him to build up the stamina to run fifty-eight marathons after the age of fifty-five. Focus is an indicative trait of a waymaker. Waymakers, however, maintain focus on things that are equally as important to them as they are self-improving. Not all waymakers will highlight fitness and abundant reading as areas of interest, but they will find areas of self-improvement to focus on, as opposed to focusing on time-wasting alternatives.

Pat also thinks the highest compliment someone can receive is "when someone tells another person they are well read." Pat also prefers "real books" as opposed to the digital versions of books popular today, saying, "I want to hold the book in my hand. I want to turn the pages. I want to have a pen close by that I can mark and bracket something that I want to save or keep."

Not surprisingly, Pat added, "I love to visit bookstores. Everybody has a happy place, or should, in their life. It might be a park bench. It might be a favorite restaurant. Maybe an ice cream shop. Could be any place. My happy spot is a Barnes & Noble. If I have time, if I'm having kind of a slow day, or if I need to get happy, I end up at the nearest Barnes & Noble. That's where I'm most comfortable. That's where I'm the happiest." The extreme volume of Pat's reading doesn't come without issue, however, as longtime lead sports columnist for the *Orlando Sentinel* Larry Guest jokingly tells others: "If you could turn Pat's books back into trees, we could reforest the great Northwest."

Two Types of Libraries

As previously mentioned, the Pat Williams Leadership Library is currently under construction. An entire wing of the First Baptist church in Orlando, where Pat is a member, will be housing the collection. Long an idea in his mind, the project really began to take shape upon his retirement from the Orlando Magic and the NBA in 2019. Prior to grabbing hold of a vision to bring an MLB baseball team to Orlando, Pat had dreams of accomplishing a few legacy projects postretirement. In true waymaker fashion, this library would be the first of his plans to use his final years to give back as much as he can to others.

In this case, Pat is gifting more than thirty thousand books to the library. Each book, which have all been previously owned and read by Pat, will then be cataloged by the church. "It's going to be a massive amount of work," Pat said before thinking about the exponential growth of the project. "That library keeps growing because more books keep coming out, and I'm always tempted to dive into the new ones. I've got close to seven hundred books here at home that I'm behind on."

Those books will soon be on display and available for future generations of Orlando residents, displayed along with Pat's vast collection of sports memorabilia. Pat has a clear vision for what he sees the library becoming, saying, "I would like it to be a place for research. I would like it to be a place where people could come and reflect. I would like it to be a place where people could come and, maybe more than anything, get excited about the art and the gift of reading. We're going to make it very clear that I have read all these books over seventy years, and I want people to gasp. I want them to be overwhelmed. And above all, I want them to leave saying, 'Reading is what I need to be doing.'"

While progress began on the library in 2019, the church had hopes of opening within twelve months, but COVID-19 has slowed its progress indefinitely. Danny DeArmas is one of the pastors at First Baptist Orlando and doesn't know exactly when the library will open but certainly knows why the church wants to house the collection. He said, "Pat says often that 'leaders read,' and that's an important part of what it means: to lead is to read. So we wanted to highlight that theme and his years of dedicated leadership."

Danny added, "He's been a member of our church for a long time and a great community leader right here in central Florida. He's influenced the community here and stood as a follower of Jesus in a winsome way, in a secular setting, and he's done a really beautiful job of that. We want to honor that and also inspire our leaders here to be leaders like Pat."

For years prior to planting the Pat Williams Leadership Library in Orlando, Pat has been practicing building libraries in people's homes, albeit on a much smaller scale. Pat has a habit of handing out trunk books from his car upon meeting a friend for a meal or mailing close friends and colleagues his newest release. So many of those close to

Pat have acquired enough books to house their own tinier versions of the Pat Williams Leadership Library.

Former MLB player and manager Bob Boone said, "Pat and I have been close friends for a long time. Well, I've had the opportunity to have every one of his books in my library, all one hundred of them or more. I'm getting two and three every time I see him."

Bob, drafted by the Phillies in 1969, met Pat while he was GM of the Philadelphia 76ers. They became close, however, when the two became involved in the same Christian education group. In one of Pat's failed paths to bring baseball to Orlando in the 1990s, Pat used some of his friendship currency, a term we will unpack further in a future chapter, to hire his friends Denny Doyle and Bob Boone to be the general manager and manager of the team, respectively. Bob said, "On an off day in Kansas City, where I played my last year, we whipped down and had a press conference with Pat naming me the manager of the nonexistent team in Orlando."

Pat once sent his book *How to Be the Ultimate Teammate* to his friend and coach Steve Fisher before it was released. The book featured a section on NBA player Jameer Nelson that college and pro basketball coach Steve thought would be relevant to share with his players. He said, "I remember watching Jameer when he played for St. Joseph's, and I really liked the way he played. And then the way Pat described him as that ultimate teammate, it was something that we could all learn from. All your players talk a good game, but how can you be a great teammate? What's involved? How do you have to think?"

Steve has coached a number of successful teams including the University of Michigan men's basketball 1988–89 national title team, as well as the famous Fab Five team—which went to back-to-back championship games and included players Chris Webber, Jalen Rose, and Juwan Howard. Steve said Pat's book was "significant" as well as "mandated reading for our players going on road trips. Every player on our team knew who Pat Williams was because every player on our team read at least part of *How to Be the Ultimate Teammate*."

By adding to the home libraries of his friends and colleagues, it seems the messages in Pat's books have even found a way to lead those who don't know Pat personally. The ability to positively influence someone's life without having to be present in it is evidence of a successful waymaker.

MLB executive Charlie Evranian said, "He always sends me a copy of the different books that he writes with a little passage in it." Charlie, who worked under Pat's mentor Bill Veeck while he was with the Chicago White Sox, said, "I really enjoyed his book *Unsinkable* about going through life and not letting everything latch on to you and pull you down and hold you back. How to cut those cords and move on with your life and don't sit and wallow, so to speak. That spoke to me."

Charlie also has the unique position of being one of the rare times Pat's friendship currency went unspent. "When he went to the Bulls, he called me at the end of our baseball season and said, 'I want you to come to Chicago and be my business manager.' Pat flew me into Chicago. We spent a lot of time together, figured out where we would live, what the salary was and everything. I said, 'I need two months to fulfill this obligation with major league baseball, and then I'll be back.' Pat said, 'I've got to have you immediately. That's the deal.'" Wanting to keep his commitments with MLB, Charlie was unable to connect with Pat on this opportunity.

Years later, Pat found a different way to act as a waymaker in Charlie's life. "There've been times when I've been a little bit down on my luck and we would talk and he'd give me an encouragement,"

Charlie said. "Some of it was faith based. He would always tell me in his different notes to me, the last line was always 'Hang in there, things are going to get better for you.' He was always encouraging."

Perhaps the greatest example of Pat influencing Charlie's life came in 1968, when Pat invited him to attend a Fellowship of Christian Athletes banquet. At the event, Pat spoke and shared a poem by an unknown author called "The Master's Face." Upon returning home, Charlie asked Pat for a copy of the poem. "I memorized it," Charlie said after receiving a copy. "I would use it a lot when I would speak at youth groups," he said.

"The poem keeps me grounded. I repeat it today when I get carried away with myself. It was a very inspiring thing that Pat invoked upon me. And probably the only piece of literature I put to memory in my life," Charlie said about the significance of the poem. Charlie then shared the entire poem from memory and concluded his monologue with a line that closely resembles the description of a waymaker: "My thoughts are now for the souls of my fellow man. I've lost my life to find it again. E'er since one day in a quiet place, I met the master face to face." ★

CHAPTER ELEVEN

WRITE A BOOK

From the Mind to the Page

In today's entrepreneurial world culture, nearly everyone who wants to be an expert in their field has authored a book. The rise of technology has allowed this practice to become easier than ever before. Instead of trying to find a publisher to help you write and market your story, self-publishing or vanity printings exist to get your book into the marketplace for an upfront cost. For those who choose to take the DIY approach, Amazon and other places offer print-on-demand services to turn your Word document into an e-book.

On average, a new book is available for purchase on Amazon every five minutes. Many leaders and influencers use their book more as a business card than as an expression of their passion on a subject. Pat, however, was authoring books as a leader in his field long before the idea could be seen on page 1 of countless branding and marketing companies' handbooks for entrepreneurs.

Pat said, "Leadership has become such a big topic in our country. There are endless numbers of seminars, retreats, conferences, or gatherings. So many people are out there talking and teaching. At every university in America now, you can get a degree and an advanced degree in leadership. That doesn't even take into account the books that are pouring out monthly on this topic of leadership. It just is absolutely unbelievable.

"Now, when I grew up all the way up into my adult years, I don't remember any books on leadership. I don't remember anybody talking about it. You did it, but I don't remember anybody saying, 'Now, here are three principles of leadership that I want you to be thinking about.' That never happened. That never came up, but now it's a huge industry unto itself."

As of this writing, Pat has authored 113 books, with another one due to be released in early 2021 called *Revolutionary Leadership*. "In this book," Pat says, "we take a look at all the leaders of the Revolutionary War period and relate how, through their efforts, our country was born. And that if any one of those men and women had not been there at that time, we might not have a country today.

"I write primarily about leadership, teamwork, winning and being successful in life, and I've focused a great deal on individuals who we view as great leaders," he continued. "I've written a series on leadership. *Bear Bryant on Leadership*. *Bobby Bowden on Leadership*. We did *Tom Osborne on Leadership*. We did *Vince Lombardi on Leadership*. *Walt Disney on Leadership*. I'm fascinated with this whole area of leadership."

Years ago, after only authoring a few dozen books, Pat set a new goal to author one hundred books. He assembled a small team to help him reach that goal. After more than a decade, he succeeded. Crossing that finish line, however, didn't seem to slow down the eighty-year-old Pat, as new titles continued to be published each year.

Longtime Atlanta Braves GM John Schuerholz—who is only a few months younger than Pat—talked about what it takes to keep contributing at that age, saying, "We just keep driving. We love what we do, and we think, 'I can still add value or creativity.'" In regard to Pat's continued efforts to write new books as opposed to playing golf and relaxing more, John said, "Most people sit down to have breakfast in the morning; he sits down to write a book."

Pat's journey to write a book begins with an idea. A good example is when he traveled to West Point, the United States Military Academy, and noticed granite benches located on campus. Each bench was etched with a different word on its side. Pat took those twelve words—which included *compassion*, *courage*, and *dedication*—and wrote chapters telling the stories of military men and women who personified those traits to create the book *Character Carved in Stone*.

Other titles come from Pat's desire to see how other people achieve and accomplish incredible things in their lives. Dozens of sports stars, coaches, and politicians have been the subject of a Pat Williams book. Of all the men and women Pat has written about in the last several decades, Walt Disney stands tallest among them. Having written multiple books on the subject of Disney, there is no doubt that Pat has a deep love and respect for the vision and work of Orlando's original visionary.

Pat said, "When I moved [to Orlando] thirty-four years ago, like many people, I got 'Disneyized.' I got hooked. I began to have these wonderful experiences at Disney concerts and meetings. Fun times. I became fascinated with Walt Disney himself, and I began to run into senior Disney executives who had worked with Walt Disney back in

California years before. In those settings, I would always pick their brains. 'Tell me: What did you learn from Walt? What are the qualities that set Walt apart? What made him a great leader? What secrets from Walt's life can you share with me?'"

Pat continued, "They were always very, very generous, and so eventually I began to speak about what I learned. Groups would come in, and I would talk about Disney's five secrets of success. Eventually that led to a book called *Go for the Magic*. We wanted to go deeper, though, and that led to the book *How to Be Like Walt*—which is still out there. I still hear from people about that one. It has been translated into many of the world's major languages. Most recently, we did *Lead Like Walt*, where we studied Walt strictly through the narrow lens of leadership."

Professional Storyteller

Pat's writing efforts have become a greater part of his day-to-day work in recent decades. At his peak, Pat was releasing an average of four books a year, a workload that only a waymaker pushing himself to go the extra mile could do. Pat said, "It requires an enormous amount of phoning and tracking down people who would have known Bear Bryant, John Wooden, Walt Disney, et cetera. There's research that has to be done. It's pleasurable work for me. I enjoy doing that research and learning so much, but eventually I hired Jim Denney on the West Coast to help me pull it all together and make sense of it all."

"We were introduced in late 1994," Jim said about the beginning of his work with Pat. "He had already done a number of books working with Jerry Jenkins. Jerry had moved on to write the Left Behind series, and Pat was looking for another writer to work with. He was full of ideas and easy to work with. He sent me a carton full of notes on three-by-five cards, and we had a lot of conversations in which we hammered out the shape and contents of the book. I didn't know it then, but that was the beginning of a writing partnership that would last for more than twenty-five years and continues to this day."

Jim and Pat have written around fifty titles together since then. They were introduced by an editor at Thomas Nelson named Janet Thoma. Janet said, "Pat wrote originally for Thomas Nelson Publishing. I was an editorial vice president there. He used to credit me with being the one who got him writing books and books and books because I would always tell him, 'If you get an idea, or you get a story, write it down, Pat. Put it somewhere, and when you need it, it will be there.'"

"I called her the piranha," Pat said about Janet, "because she would criticize your work if she wasn't happy." Janet, who was aware of her nickname, admitted, "I did sort of have that reputation, but an editor is really a reader's friend. We work with an author to make sure there is nothing there that doesn't go along with the main theme of the book. I did cut so much out of his books, I have to admit."

While Janet helped bring Jim and Pat together, their long-lasting partnership has produced more titles than most single authors could ever hope to write in a lifetime. Spending that much time with a waymaker has certainly impacted Jim's life.

Jim said, "Whenever I work on a book with Pat, he teaches me something. He teaches me about success, about faith, about character. I worked with him on a book about his journey through multiple myeloma, *The Mission Is Remission: Hope for Battling Cancer*. I interviewed Pat, his wife, his doctors, his sister, and many other people who went through that journey with him. He spoke candidly about his fears at the beginning of the treatment. He let me into his life in a way that showed me what courage and faith really look like. Working with Pat is always an adventure and an education. With many of the decisions I've made in my own life and career, I've asked myself, 'What would Pat Williams do in this situation?'"

Pat's biggest priority when writing a book is to fill it with as many stories as he can, saying, "There's got to be at least one story on either one of those two pages [a reader has opened] because when people's eyes focus on a story, they are going to stay with you. I love to see quotation marks. If I see nothing but dry words and charts and graphs, for example, I move on."

NBA player turned executive Pat Garrity—who played nine seasons with the Magic—said the thing that stood out most to him about Pat was that he was "an exceptional storyteller." He continued, "That manifested in the number of books he wrote, but I think he understands the power of conveying stories to people to teach deeper messages or truths. It showed in his dedication to go out and continually trying to be on the lookout to find the best stories and the best way to convey them to the broadest audience."

During his career, Pat's large number of published books on a variety of topics have caused him to be a highly booked public speaker. In addition to speaking on the circuit, Pat will often travel to do press tours for his books. He has been invited onto radio and television programs across the country to promote various titles. One of his favorite spots to visit during his promotional tours is the big Barnes & Noble on Park Avenue in New York City.

Cal Hunter—who handles the business development for the Barnes & Noble on Fifth Avenue—has become another member of Pat's friendship collection and talked about the impact his books have had on readers, saying, "Pat's experienced a lot personally. Those are the things that gravitate us toward each other, connect us, and remind us that we have to be about something bigger than ourselves. We have to be able to see the plight of someone else and, where we can, make a difference."

Pat didn't start writing as a business decision to improve his brand. Instead, Pat sees books as an opportunity to learn something for himself that he can then pass on to someone else. Waymakers are always concerning themselves with this type of work. Being a lifelong learner is a great ideal to strive for, but using that wisdom to become a lifelong teacher may be even greater.

Pat has interviewed thousands of the most prominent names of our generations. He has researched the world's greatest leaders. He has studied those who have done unbelievable things to learn how they did it. Every book he has written since is Pat's summation on his findings. He can't make us explore the lessons he has to teach, but he has certainly left a large trail of his books behind for us to learn from if we choose to discover what he found. ★

★ ★ ★

CHAPTER TWELVE

CREATE FRIENDSHIP CURRENCY

Making Connections

In Malcom Gladwell's book *The Tipping Point*, he describes the type of person in communities who knows a large number of individuals and habitually makes introductions. Gladwell calls these types of people *connectors*. Connectors have an extraordinary knack for making friends and acquaintances. Pat Williams is a benchmark connector. Over the years, he has used his genuine friendships to help his friends and acquaintances get connected with the right person or opportunity.

Pat's childhood friend Ruly Carpenter was perhaps the first significant connection, a relationship soldered in grade school nearly seven decades ago. Ruly knows, more than most, the value of having Pat in your life. "We were classmates and teammates for quite a number of years," Ruly said prior to sharing more details about how they have stayed close for so long.

"After we graduated from high school, we went our separate ways. He went to Wake Forest, and I went to Yale University. We maintained continual contact, and then Pat worked for the Phillies as the general manager of the Spartanburg team," said Ruly, whose family owned the Phillies at the time.

Long after Pat worked for the Phillies for seven years, however, he maintained a close connected relationship with his best friend from grade school. "I've always considered him a great, very loyal personal friend. And a very knowledgeable guy from the management end of sports," Ruly said. He added, "When he was with the Sixers, we were in contact constantly during the season. They were right across the street, really. He'd come over to the [Phillies] games and sit there with me and our folks and watch the games. And it was just a great relationship." To this day, whenever Pat visits the Philadelphia area, he stays in the guest room at Ruly's home.

Staying in a childhood friend's home while traveling may be atypical waymaker behavior but also sheds light on both the long-lasting bond Pat creates with his friends and the value he places on staying connected with them.

Brian Kilmeade is the host of a popular cable news program called *Fox and Friends*. Friendship currency has connected Brian and Pat numerous times over the course of their friendship. Brian, who has had Pat as a guest on his show nearly twenty-five times, knows that Pat stands out as an exemplary waymaker in a nation of great leaders, saying, "Pat was the only person I knew that achieved what he achieved and asked more questions about me than I asked him. I'm always fascinated by how he listens and remembers."

At first, Brian questioned if Pat was really this nice a person or if it was an act, but after Pat took the time over the years to send thoughtful notes and voice mails, Brian said, "He grades through the roof on how you treat people you need nothing from. Over the years, he's one of the people I could always look up to."

Years before Pat was a regular guest on *Fox and Friends*, Pat was the first person Brian thought to interview when he started writing his first book, *The Games Do Count*. He said, "I interviewed seventy-three people. I knew Pat's story a little and thought his success in sports helped set him up for life. So I go down to Orlando with my son to meet Pat. We're talking on the court after an Orlando Magic game. There were people slamming the seats and stacking the chairs. I was glad I was taping the interview because it was so loud. I didn't have the guts to ask if we can move somewhere else because I couldn't believe he was giving me the time. Sure enough, when I get back, I realized I couldn't transcribe it."

A defeated Brian needed to call Pat and ask if he would graciously do another interview. Brian shared the impact of that call, saying, "Pat, of course, said, 'No problem.' We hit the ground running, and it was even better the second time. I thought, 'For Pat to care so much for a guy he doesn't hardly know was unbelievable.'"

Brian, who also coached a high-level soccer team for twenty-four seasons, recalled another moment where Pat was the right connection needed for a particular moment, saying, "Our team went to Florida. I asked Pat if he would come speak to the players between games. He treated it like I was Microsoft offering him $150,000 for a forty-five-minute speech. He asked about the team, their families, what the sport means to them, and what they were planning to accomplish. It was pretty amazing to see the level of detail Pat put into a favor."

Boston Globe sports columnist Bob Ryan first connected with Pat in 1970, while traveling with the Boston Celtics. Bob said, "I can't pinpoint our first encounter, but baseball is our big bond," before sharing about a treasured moment with Pat. "It's the NBA Finals in

1980. The 76ers are playing the Lakers, and I'm covering the series for the *Boston Globe*."

He continued, "It was the week of the baseball draft, and *Sports Illustrated* had first made known the name of Darryl Strawberry. At the hotel, I had finished my writing for the day and was headed for the pool when the phone rang. Pat said, 'Darryl Strawberry is playing at Crenshaw High School today. I got directions. Let's go.'

"We positioned ourselves in the bleachers on the first base side. We identify Darryl without a program. During the game, Darryl gets a couple hits and stole second base with a beautiful pop-up slide." Bob shared how that was a highlight moment for him as a baseball fan and confessed that he "retained the Marriot legal notepad I used to write the directions on. I saved it all these years." He added, "My relationship with Pat is special. I've had good acquaintances with a lot of people over the years, but nothing like this. This is a true friendship."

Paying Dividends

Karly Kirkpatrick met Pat in the summer of 2006 as an intern for the Orlando Magic marketing department. "He would get talking and seemed to take a real interest in me," Karly said about her initial interactions with Pat. "I was a soccer player, and my dad played in the NFL. He loved the sports aspect of my family, and he became my mentor right away."

As a mentor, Pat would leave marketing books for Karly in her mailbox with highlighted passages he thought would help her. He also encouraged her to pursue a master's degree. Similar to internal questions posed by Brian Kilmeade about Pat's authenticity, Karly thought, "Why does Pat care about me? I'm just an intern." It didn't take her long to learn he was doing the same thing for her she saw him do for so many others.

"I get goosebumps about Pat because he made such an impact in my life," Karly went on to say. After getting fired from the Magic—a common occurrence among all positions in the world of professional sports—Karly said Pat was the first person to reach out to her, saying, "He asked me what I was planning on doing, but I wasn't sure. He said, 'No, we need a plan. You need to stay in sports.' The next day, I have somebody calling me from the New York Yankees organization. When I asked how they got my number, they said 'Pat Williams.'"

Karly, who later married Chris Kirkpatrick from the band NSYNC, invited Pat to give a blessing and pray at her wedding, which included Justin Timberlake and other celebrity guests. "He was like a father figure to me," Karly said about the honor she wanted to give Pat as opposed to any of the other prominent guests in attendance. In Pat's eyes, Karly was as valuable as a person who was interning as she is today, an idea not lost on Karly. She said, "It shows how special Pat is because he traveled to pray at the wedding for one of his interns."

Tara McClary Reeves is a mother and author from Virginia whose parents were friends with Pat way back in the 1960s. "I had the advantage of Pat kind of adopting me too," Tara said about her earliest memories of interactions with Pat. "He would send me a stack of books that he had gone through and highlighted with his notes in the margins. He would also send me a newspaper article about something in history that he doesn't want me to forget."

Years later, Pat, who has always lovingly looked out for Tara as a father figure, called her one day and said, "Tara, I just met your husband." Tara, who had long been waiting for God's best for her life and did not want to settle, laughed before asking Pat, "Okay, who is it?" Pat replied, "His name is Lee Reeves." Tara, who had previously known Lee because their families were acquaintances who exchanged Christmas cards, went on to say that "Pat had made that reconnection for the man that would ultimately become my husband."

Most recently, Pat has been encouraging Tara to get into the world of politics, telling her, "Tara, there is not one female politician that can hold a candle to you right now." While unsure about her future in politics, Tara did say that after a conversation with Pat, "you feel like you can conquer the world. While I weigh every piece of advice he gives me against the word of God, it's nice to have a coach and cheerleader who looks after you and has a vision for you."

Opportunities Not Handouts

While Tara may or may not be considering a run in politics, Pat's longtime friend John Ashcroft has made politics a career. "He has been a friend to me. He is, in my estimation, a fine Christian gentleman, who has the ability to inspire people," John said about his relationship with Pat. He went on to describe how Pat was not only an effective planner in his own life but could also "help people plan." Whether for himself or others, John said Pat knew how "to make plans for good things to happen and then make them happen."

> "[Pat] is a person of integrity and morality and compassion for other people, and that draws other people to him."

When asked how Pat exemplifies his Christian faith, John said, "The first thing that comes to mind is the Boy Scout oath. Trustworthy, loyal, helpful, friendly, courteous, kind, obedient, cheerful, thrifty, brave, clean, and reverent. He is a person of integrity and morality and compassion for other people, and that draws other people to him." There may be many reasons Pat is a connector, but the Boy Scout oath definitely hits on several key characteristics that apply to Pat's life. Friends, especially ones you let advise or influence your life in a positive way, will usually have a variety of traits that need to be expressed to another person in order to be effective. For example, being friendly, courteous, or kind, as the Boy Scout oath states, needs the participation of at least two people because it's difficult to be courteous to yourself.

Characteristics that require two parties to activate, such as helpfulness, trustworthiness, and loyalty, can be attributed to Pat, and likely many other waymakers, because waymakers cannot become waymakers without being a good friend.

Marci Doyle, for example, has known Pat since she was a little girl. Marci's father, Denny Doyle, was a star of the Spartanburg team that Pat managed in the late 1960s. Marci said, "They were fast friends. Pat was the young GM doing all these crazy promotions and programs. Dad was the young star they were all coming to see."

Denny Doyle went on to play in the major leagues with the Phillies, Angels, and Red Sox. In the late '80s, Pat headed to Orlando to start the Magic, and Denny, who had finished his career in the majors, came to town as well to start the Doyle Baseball School. "My sister and brother-in-law babysat his kids. Three or four of his boys came through Doyle Academy," Marci said about the closeness of the two families.

Marci eventually found herself both watching and later benefiting from Pat's waymaker life, saying, "Pat was wonderful for me as a mentor because everybody needs people that are willing to help you out early in your career. He was the first one that said, 'What do you want to do?' and 'How can I help you?' He was so encouraging. He actually set up a couple of interviews for me. I ended up getting an internship with the AA Orlando Sun Rays one summer when I was still in college."

While many may see Pat's helpfulness in providing an internship to a family friend, Marci learned a valuable lesson on the reality behind help like that. She said, "He told me, 'Don't ever feel badly about utilizing contacts and networks. You still have to prove yourself. All they're doing is opening a door. You still have to prove that you've earned it and you can do the work.'"

Marci continued, "I was very much against using anyone my dad knew or any contact he had in the sports industry. I wanted to prove it and do it myself, and Pat went, 'No, no, no. Let me clarify. That's not how you need to do it. You need to take advantage of that. That is not a handout. That's called an opportunity, and you still have to prove yourself.'"

Later, Marci was the longtime tournament director and COO for the Arnold Palmer Invitational Professional Golfers' Association (PGA) tour event in Orlando. While using Pat's friendship currency to get her foot in the door may not have been her initial choice, she said her first internship through Pat was "kind of my start into sports and entertainment management and marketing. That was my first taste of it, and I never looked back."

Another example of Pat giving someone an opportunity and not a handout comes from Kelly Lafferman. She, too, was the recipient of an Orlando Sun Rays internship, afforded because of that relationship Pat had with Kelly's mom, who was the chair for the World Cup soccer committee in Orlando. "I was a sports marketing major at Florida State and was really interested in getting into the sports business," Kelly said about her opportunity.

Kelly said she quickly found out "baseball is the hardest thing you can ever work in. If you can work in minor-league baseball, you can pretty much do anything. That was my first real gig, and then I went and worked for the Olympics in Atlanta." After the Olympics, Pat helped Kelly land a marketing job with the Magic, where later she was part of the team that launched the WNBA Orlando Miracle.

Pat played a big waymaker role for Kelly, not because he did good work for her, but rather because he afforded her the opportunity to do that good work herself. Now in her fifties, Kelly talked about how Pat was a "good role model" because "that was when I was in my twenties. To see somebody be personally interested in you when you're at the bottom of the totem pole and he's at the top. To care about everybody and want to know their fears, their strengths, and everything. He would use your quotes and stories in his own speeches, and he'd write them down on cards. He made you feel like you were important."

One unique situation that really highlights how Pat offers opportunities instead of handouts came when Jeanette Hughes was invited to stay with the Williams family. Jeanette was a hairdresser-turned-pageant-trainer for Pat's daughter Karyn. After meeting Pat at Karyn's first pageant—where she was first runner-up—Jeanette said, "We became great friends. I was traveling all the time. When I would come back to Orlando, they insisted I stayed at their house. So I lived in their house for ten years. Once a month."

Jeanette traveled between Orlando and her home in Myrtle Beach, South Carolina, because she had sold her salon practice but rented a space in Orlando to cut hair one week a month. While staying with the Williamses, Jeanette would cut the family's hair and sometimes eat meals with them. She believes she was afforded this generosity while training Karyn. She said, "I made a lot of her clothes and became a big part of the family, and it became a really nice trusting and friendly relationship."

Friendships are the currency of a waymaker. As a connector, Pat uses his relationships to become a waymaker that helps open doors, encourage, and make paths for others. His relationship with Brian inspired a young soccer team. With Karly, he helped her become a candidate for a new job in sports. Pat also used his friendship currency to help Tara find a husband and give me—an unknown writer—the opportunity to write this book. ★

CHAPTER THIRTEEN

PRACTICE EMPATHY

The Special Ingredient

Great relationships are built upon mutual trust, respect, and compassion for one another. Trailblazers may not always take the time to share their feelings with others. Instead, you may find a trailblazer exhibiting ruthlessness, greed, and selfishness while they are on their way to the top. A waymaker, however, can not only find the time to share in the feelings of a friend but often makes those types of connections a priority in his life.

Like so many of Pat's friends, former pro baseball scout and executive Al Goldis has known Pat for decades. Their introduction, however, may be the most unusual in this book. Al, who played in the minor leagues with the Reds organization in the '60s, shared a story about a game he played against Pat's Miami Marlins team, saying, "I was the on-deck hitter. We had a guy on second base, and his name was Tom Perdue, who in all my career was probably the toughest human being I've ever been around. The hitter before me hit a line drive to right field. The right fielder was a fellow by the name of Hank Allen. His brother Dick Allen had played in the big leagues. Hank threw a perfect one-hopper to the catcher. Tom rounded third and was coming in to hit the plate. He had this look like the Hulk, and he hit the catcher so hard he broke the catcher's thigh bone. Who came in the game to replace him? Pat Williams."

Over the years, Al has gotten to know Pat off the field and said, "Besides his intelligence, empathy is the key to why he is so successful. I think the special ingredient that he has is his understanding and empathy for people. You get things done through people when you treat them with respect. You treat them the way you want to be treated or the way you want your kids to be treated. I think he put that into actual behavior. That's the way he lived."

NBA Hall of Famer Nancy Lieberman has interacted with a lot of the same people as Pat over the years. "There's enough people we have to work with that we don't want to be around on a daily basis, but Pat is the type of guy you actually do want to interact with. You always leave a conversation with him feeling better, relaxed and free, like he actually cares about you."

She added, "We could talk about life. We can talk about love. We can talk about faith. We can talk about children, grandkids. There is nothing he's not willing to talk to you about. He's availed himself to people like me every day. He is a mentor. He has tremendous wisdom. He has empathy. He has a really great business mind. If you've come in contact with him over the years, you're better off for it, because he not only has wisdom, but he shares it. There's a lot of great people in the world, some are rich and have a high IQ, some have great experiences, but if you're not willing to share it, it's not worth having."

Not only has Pat been an empathetic mentor in Nancy's life, but she has seen him do the same for so many others. She said, "Pat has affected a lot of people's lives, and he's kind of an under-the-radar guy. You're not going to walk around the streets and go, 'Hey, there's Pat Williams,' but if you ask the circle that he has walked in during his life, he's a superhero."

Learn by Example

Empathy, like many of Pat's high-quality traits and abilities, was exemplified for him at an early age by his parents. Pat remembered a time his mother got his mind off baseball and thinking about the hopes and dreams of others. "It was August of 1963; I had just finished my second year as a ballplayer in Miami. I was heading home up the East Coast to Wilmington, Delaware. My mother said, 'We're going to be at this event in Washington; why don't you just meet us there?' I agreed to meet my family, little realizing that it would be one of the great moments in American history."

Pat continued, "I joined them catty-corner to the main stage. Sure enough, that was the day Dr. Martin Luther King Jr. delivered his famous 'I Have a Dream' speech. That was a great moment in my life. I learned the power of the spoken word when delivered by a gifted orator, and that's what Dr. King was."

Pat's parents, James and Ellen, were also civic leaders who helped to raise awareness and funding for Down syndrome children via the Blue-Gold All-Star exhibition game fundraiser each August. Pat once said, "My dad's greatest moment took place in the first year of that all-star game."

Pat continued, "It was the summer of 1956. The northern part of the state would play against players from the southern part of the state. The northern team was going to train for two weeks at a prep school outside of Wilmington, Sanford Prep. There were two Black players that made the northern squad—Alvin Hall and Joe Peters. We ran into a problem. Sanford Prep said, 'It's all right if these two guys practice and eat here, but we've got students from the South. We think they would be very uncomfortable if these two players stayed here overnight.'"

Pat went on to say, "My dad, who was a product of Greensboro, North Carolina, and the University of North Carolina, stood up and said, 'No problem. These two guys will stay at our house, and my son Pat will be their chauffeur.' And that's what happened. That might've been one of my dad's finest hours. For two weeks I drove Alvin and Joe out to practice early in the morning and picked them up in the evening. That was the first time I ever got to become friends with African American guys."

Pat's mother, Ellen, also presented lessons for Pat to practice his empathy. One example occurred after a tragic accident involving a family member of one of Pat's Wake Forest teammates, Bobby Brown. Bobby remembered, "Pat and his family are really the kind of people that we need more of in this country and in this world. They're super people. I feel very fortunate to have had my experience with them. It's not just Pat, but with his mom and his dad, particularly his mom.

Waymakers see people. They see their hopes and their dreams, but they also see their pain and their hurts.

"When my father was killed after being hit by an automobile, Pat and his mom made an effort to come down and visit with my mother and myself—which I thought was way out of the norm, but it's worth mentioning for me." The impact of practiced empathy still is a fresh memory in Bobby's mind more than fifty years later and is evidence of why empathy is a commonly found trait among waymakers.

Waymakers see people. They see their hopes and their dreams, but they also see their pain and their hurts. Waymakers aren't only interested in giving advice that helps people succeed but also to be a hand to hold or a shoulder to cry on during those vulnerable moments in life we all face.

Seeing People

Longtime Orlando Magic broadcaster David Steele remembers a package he received from Pat after the loss of his mother to leukemia. He said, "They were trying to convince me to make a decision to leave the [Florida] Gators and come to Orlando. It was in November 1988, right before Thanksgiving, and I'll never forget that I got a note from Pat. A really nice handwritten note and a little book on dealing with the loss of a loved one."

David continued, "It was a very personal note and just spot on. It was something that was just over and above what you would expect anybody to do in a situation like that, and it made a big impression on me. You know that this was somebody that was a caring person. A quality person. Somebody that was more than just looking at it from a business standpoint. He was trying to hire good people and people that he thought would fit the organization. So that was a big factor in me responding positively in January. I took the offer, and I've had a great relationship with Pat from the very beginning."

NFL coach Andy Reid has also been on the receiving end of Pat's notes of encouragement. This recent-Super-Bowl-winning coach said, "When things are good, he'll send me a note and say congratulations. But during the low times, whether it's dealing with my family or with my son's death or with losses like an AFC [American Football Conference] or NFC [National Football Conference] championship, he'd reach out to encourage. He's always been there through the highs and the lows.

"Like the great people can," Andy said about Pat's personal attention, "he makes you feel like you're the only one. If you step back and think about it, you're probably one of thousands. It's a unique ability he has."

Pat's friend and professional counselor Dwight Bain is one of the leading national trainers in the field of community crisis. For waymakers, empathy is so necessary when guiding those in crisis. Dwight has firsthand knowledge of what it takes when helping others and offers insight into his friend Pat.

Dwight said, "Pat was in Philadelphia, he was in Atlanta, he was in Chicago, and then he was back in Philadelphia. He was in Spartanburg, he was in Miami, but he's been in Orlando over thirty years because this is the place where he put down roots. Remember, Pat was in the army; his experiences at Wake Forest and other places broadened his sense of what is commonly called *CQ*.

"CQ is *cultural intelligence*," Dwight said as he continued to delve deep into the reasons behind Pat's profound impact on the lives of others. "*IQ* is intelligence. *EQ* is emotional awareness, and Pat has one of the highest EQs I think I've ever seen. But *CQ*—you're going to be hearing a lot more about CQ. It's being able to say 'I see people.'

"When you look at Pat's kids, they're from all over the world. His house is the United Nations, because these kids are from every major hemisphere. I think Antarctica got a pass because I don't think he could find any kids to adopt in Antarctica." Dwight added, "Jesus didn't see packaging. He saw people; He saw potential. Jesus saw underneath the skin. So because of Pat's travels and his position in the army and because of his relationship with pro sports and people, he's really good at meeting people.

"I remember the first time that I was able to get a lunch with this luminary guy, and you know, I'm young, and I had a radio show, and I was nervous. And I'll never forget—we went to an Olive Garden, and I can remember it like it was yesterday because Pat's always been health conscious.

"Pat said to the server, 'Listen, here's what I want you to do. I want a chicken breast. I want it grilled. I want some marinara sauce on the side, and I want some steamed broccoli. Can you do that?'" Shocked by the exchange between Pat and the server, Dwight said, "I think it was the first time I ever saw someone, without being rude or condescending, just tell the server, 'This is exactly what I want.'"

Dwight continued, "Remember, Pat's a marathoner, and he said exactly what he wanted, and the server said, 'Yes.' And I said, 'I think I want the Tour of Italy,' and I'm just ordering off the menu. Pat Williams doesn't use a menu because he doesn't need the menu. He already knows what he wants. When he looks at people, he doesn't go with the label. He already knows what he wants, and he's able to look at a person. I'm talking about seeing potential, and he'd be able to draw that piece out.

"So I'm sitting at this table with my Tour of Italy and my bread-sticks and my soup and salad. Pat's just eating healthy, and I've got this embarrassingly long list of questions that I wanted to ask him that I don't think I've asked him yet because he asked all the questions.

"I've learned this from Pat," Dwight continued. "You go to a meeting like that, and you have a list of questions mapped out, and he asked me questions the whole time. He knew a lot about me, my life and my story. I don't think I knew anything about him except his name was Pat Williams and he doesn't have to order off a menu.

"He is interested in people, and that deep interest in people flows through questions. Since then, I've asked him about it, and I said, 'How do you do that?' And he said, 'I'm just really curious about people. I'm really interested in people. I want to hear their story.'" Dwight summed up his observation of Pat's high-level empathy, saying, "Don't you think that Jesus was that way? That people just felt like 'this person sees me.'"

Everyone Has a Book in Them

As Dwight touched on, part of Pat's empathetic ability includes the value he sees in the stories of the people he meets. Pat has often said, "Everyone has a book in them." That means everyone has a story or a special insight worth sharing with others. While several people with a gift for writing have eagerly followed Pat's advice to become a published author and share their thoughts and ideas in a book, Pat has also encouraged those without the innate desire to write to collect their powerful stories and share them with the world.

Lucas Boyce had such an encounter with Pat. Lucas said, "I met Pat in 2008 when I was working as one of their front-office executives. I was sharing with him my foster-care-to-adoption story and about how my mom had a foster care home for fifteen years and over forty foster care kids. We started talking about dreams and goals and how I had just left the White House during the Bush administration to come to the Magic."

After getting to know Lucas, his history, and his hopes for the future, Pat put on his waymaker shoes and encouraged Lucas to tell his story. Lucas remembers Pat saying, "You need to write a book and share your story." Lucas was hesitant at first, he said, because he "didn't get into either sports or politics to ever write a book. I don't know how to write a book."

Pat, however, encouraged Lucas to spend some time writing and bring the results back to him and also shared with him that "the key element of a good book is that you must have a lot of good stories in it." Lucas listened to Pat's instructions. He said, "On nights and weekends, I started to share my story and write it down." After handing his pages over to Pat sometime later, Pat introduced Lucas to a book publisher. Lucas said that his book "was published January 1, 2011, and was called *Living Proof—From Foster Care to the White House and the NBA.*"

Today, Lucas is proud of his accomplishment but knows it may never have come about without a waymaker to guide his path. He said, "I credit that Pat was the person that put it in my heart to write. I would not have been an author had he not encouraged me to write my story down and share it with people."

Lucas, whose work provides him with the opportunity to speak publicly, often shares the following Pat quote as a part of his speeches: "A good leader knows that, at the end of the day, it is not about them, it's about the positive difference they can make in others. A good servant leader leads from the front and not the back and does whatever it takes to get the job done."

The quote is Lucas's favorite of Pat's many quotable lines on leadership. More than that, however, every time Lucas shares this quote with others, it acts as a public tribute for the influence that Pat, a man Lucas calls a "dear friend" and a "mentor," has had on his life.

Room to Breathe

Pat's expression of empathy goes deeper than making sure to connect and speak with those facing a crisis or encouraging others to realize their worth to share their story. Sometimes, Pat is able to simply not be overly demanding of others while still pushing them in the direction of doing their best. Situations that pull on this thread of empathy are often woven together while Pat is traveling.

Paul Powers has been organizing men's prayer breakfast meetings in Pittsburgh, Pennsylvania, through his Men of Honor Ministries for more than two decades. In 2002, Paul brought Pat in as a guest speaker to share his faith with over five hundred men. While in town, Pat was reading the local paper and noticed the Pittsburgh Sports Museum and asked Paul, "Is there a chance we can go there before I get on a plane to go back?" Paul answered, "I don't know if we're going to have the time." Without any pressure Pat said, "It's your call, Paul."

After his speech, Paul wanted to attempt to get Pat to the museum but said, "When we hit the Parkway that goes right into Pittsburgh, there was a complete stop. So I said, 'Pat, I don't know.' He goes, 'Paul, it's okay. It's your call.' So after about three minutes, traffic starts up again, and we head over. He told me, 'This sports museum is probably the best sports museum I've ever seen.'"

While not exactly a monumental event in Paul's future, the moment, which featured Pat's desire to see history as well as his penchant for patience and understanding, left a lasting impression on Paul. Leaving the decision up to Paul to make Pat's trip to the museum a reality allowed Paul to take ownership of the day's schedule. Pat could've been demanding or angry as the guest of honor, but instead submitted to Paul's authority and schedule. Paul said, "Pat's handling of the situation made me feel really good, and I was happy he got to go through the museum."

Waymakers are always able to find ways to influence others. The great waymakers create dozens of avenues to encourage and influence, with a good piece of usable advice, a great speech, or a job opportunity often the easiest methods we can point to as evidence of a waymakers success. Moments like the one with Paul are likely more common in quantity but less notable in the history books of Pat's successes. However, these behind-the-scenes moments of practicing empathy are great examples to follow when trying to emulate the attitude and abilities of this waymaker. ★

★ ★ ★

CHAPTER FOURTEEN

OBSERVE OTHER LEADERS

A Guided Tour

Pat Williams is an expert on leadership. He observes leaders. He reads about leaders. He writes about leaders. His work involves him with other leaders at every turn. Not to mention, Pat has been a leader himself throughout his life. Therefore, it was no surprise he had such a hardline answer to my question "What is the most important quality of leadership?" He said, "Without question, it's called *vision*.

"The great leaders have the ability to see farther down the road than the rest of us. They see a finished product clearly in their minds. Visionaries work backwards to put the pieces into place, to turn their vision into reality. That's how they go about it. Visionary leaders change the world. Visionary leaders make things happen that the rest of us can't even picture," Pat said before turning into my tour guide for an exploration down a trail of great leadership examples.

"George Washington's vision during the eight long years of the Revolutionary War was a new nation, the United States of America, a nation independent of Great Britain's rule. And that's what drove Washington. Abraham Lincoln's vision during his five tough years in the White House was one nation, not two independent ones or three or five smaller ones. One nation."

Pat continued, "Winston Churchill's vision was a world free of Nazi oppression, and that's what kept him going, particularly during those early years of World War II, when Great Britain stood alone. When we look at Martin Luther King Jr., we know his vision was a nation where we would not be judged by the color of our skin but by the content of our character."

Pat then shared the early vision of John F. Kennedy by doing his best impression of the cadence of the former president's voice, saying, "I believe this nation should set a goal before this decade is out of landing a man on the moon and returning him safely to earth." Pat added a note that it was Pat's now-home in Orlando that birthed a future astronaut named John Young who appreciated Kennedy's words, specifically the part where he said "returning him safely to earth." Kennedy's vision was fulfilled in 1969 when Neil Armstrong and company made it back home safely by speaking those now-famous words—"the Eagle has landed."

Pat continued guiding the tour by highlighting Ronald Reagan, saying, "His vision from the time he got into politics was a world without communism. That was his goal, and when he became the president, he made that very clear. Reagan was asked if he had a strategy. He said, 'Yes. We win. They lose.'

"Here in Orlando," Pat continued, "we have visionaries all over the place, starting with Walt Disney—who in 1963 had a vision of a second theme park. Many said to him, 'You can't have more than one.

There's only one Grand Canyon. You can only have one Disneyland; you can't have two.' And he said, 'We need one on the East Coast.' They picked Orlando. Nobody else could begin to grasp what was on his mind, what he was thinking about, but he knew. He had the whole thing mapped out, and last year seventy-eight million people from around the world came to participate in his vision."

Pat said, "It's exciting to be around visionaries and to see them. Everybody knows Arnold Palmer as a great golfer, but he moved here right after Disney. He decided to put a stake in this little community here in central Florida and make Orlando the golf capital of the country. And it happened. Nobody quite grasped what Arnold was thinking. But he had a vision of what could take place."

Pat concluded our tour with a look at the leader of our Christian faith, saying, "Jesus was a visionary. He envisioned a new eternal home and heaven, and He was going to be there, and He was going to get it prepared. He talked about it through His three years of ministry. His disciples had a terrible time understanding it. Many people today can't get their arms around it. Jesus told us, 'In my father's house are many mansions, and I'm going to prepare a place for you. And if I go to prepare a place, I shall receive you unto myself. So that where I am, you may be also.' What a vision that is! Whew! I mean, that will clear your nostrils out. And to this day, people have a tough time grasping the significance of that vision."

Dream a Little Dream

This incredible tour was Pat's response to a simple question about what characteristic is most important in a leader. While it may seem like this type of response is rehearsed—it's not. This is how Pat talks. His Rolodex memory sparked with years of practice as a prominent speaker allows him to answer questions by telling stories with great accuracy and the fervor of an impassioned general on the battlefield. As a waymaker, the stories he shares are his lessons for others to follow. Pat has often told me the best way for people to retain information is to share it in a story, and Pat is a master storyteller.

Orlando Magic assistant GM Matt Lloyd has seen the impact of Pat's storytelling firsthand. "His presentation is so good," Matt said. "He goes into every conversation knowing the message that he is going to send in that conversation. He's so polished. You can't help but get swept into his presence, and every time you speak to him you almost leave the conversation ready to run through a wall."

Matt continued, "He always had such a great way to explain things. And he would do it by telling stories. He could remember the intimate details of every single move they made in building the Magic. You could ask him a question, and he could respond in a manner where you would take away a lesson in the story that was being told. And that is such a unique ability.

"I came to the Magic, and I really had no leadership or management experience. I always thought I was prepared for it, and it turns out that I was woefully unprepared. Pat had kind of helped me along the way in showing me the way to communicate with people and to get them to do something that maybe they didn't think they could do." Matt added, "I'm not anywhere in his same universe in terms of his capacity to communicate, but if I could be 5 percent better just from my relationship with Pat, I was going to try.

"Pat's so good at delivering messages in passing too." Matt learned about Pat's ability to act as a waymaker throughout daily life. He continued, "You'd see him at the game, and he'd always have questions like 'Where have you been? What have you been doing?' And it was always interspliced with some nugget that you could take away from the conversation. Or you'd get a phone call: 'Hey, I'm just checking in on you; hope everything's going well.' I was always so impressed by that because he didn't have to check on me. I should have been checking on him."

The character of a waymaker is built by not only observing other great leaders but by applying their practices of success to their own life. For Pat, he continually notices the best qualities of great leaders and tries to reproduce them in his own life. NBA Hall of Famer Hubie Brown spoke at great length about the character of Pat Williams.

"I don't care when you meet him; you never see him on a down day. Now that's difficult, for sure," Hubie said before describing what makes Pat a leader among leaders: "He's a 24-7 type of individual. He's constantly working on two masterpieces at the same time, whether he's a general manager or whether he's writing books that are interesting to all phases of the American population. I haven't met anyone in life who is able to carry on this energetic work ethic seven days a week and still be involved with a family of nineteen kids."

Pat is able to work and live at such breakneck speeds in part because he is no stranger to having a vision himself.

Former First Baptist Orlando pastor Jimmy Knott shares Pat's love for observing other leaders. Jimmy has used the lessons of other leaders to help him in his pastoral efforts to mentor, coach, and teach. He said, "A lot of what Pat has written on has been on leadership. I've used some of Pat's books, including *Paradox in Power* and *Leadership Excellence*, in coaching other leaders. He's a great teacher."

Pat is able to work and live at such breakneck speeds in part because he is no stranger to having a vision himself. Pat has seen several visions come to pass in his own life, including his vision to play and work in professional sports and his most notable vision to bring an NBA team to Orlando in the Magic. And most recently, Pat has shared a vision to try to found an MLB team in Orlando as well.

A few days after the official announcement, Pat excitedly told me his vision for a future that includes professional baseball in Orlando: "I've got a vision that Orlando can become a Major League Baseball town. And we're going to get started. We don't know how it's all going to come out, but I've got a vision of a beautiful state-of-the-art ballpark, and I can envision baseball presented in an Orlando style that the world's never seen. I can envision thousands of people who visit here from around the world who've never seen a ball game before, and I can envision them having the time of their life at Dreamland Field—which doesn't exist, except in my mind."

Like Reagan, JFK, or other visionaries before him, a dream doesn't come without naysayers. And Pat's vision to bring a third professional baseball team—appropriately named the Orlando Dreamers—to Florida certainly has its share of skeptics. Strangely, many of those same skeptics will be the first to tell you "If anyone could do it, however, Pat Williams could." Pat is undaunted by both the naysayers and the fact that he is facing this task while in his eighties, saying, "The Dreamers may take me a decade or more to build. But when I finish that one, I'll be in my nineties, and God will have another vision for me to pursue until I turn one hundred years old." ★

CHAPTER FIFTEEN

FIND A GOOD SPOUSE

Spend Time with the Lady

Another example of Pat's capture-listening comes from a lesson in marriage he learned from Duke basketball coach Mike Krzyzewski. Pat said, "Coach K. has three daughters, and when they wanted to get married, he asked them two questions. The first question he asked was 'Does he make you a better person?' His second question: 'Do you make him a better person? If both answers are yes, proceed. If not, hold off.'"

Pat has thought a lot about marriage over the years, having written books on the subject. Marriage is one of the small number of formidable rocky roads that Pat has traveled as a waymaker. In our conversation about marriage, Pat brought up the Krzyzewski story to highlight a key lesson for marriage he learned years ago.

He said, "The more I've studied what Coach K. said, I think it makes sense to marry a person that's rooting for you, cheering for you, uplifting you, and wants you to succeed. Someone who does not resent your success and is in your corner when things are going well or when they're not. Your all-time cheerleader. If you can find that person, that's who you want to live with. That's who you want to spend your time with. That's who you want around you."

> It makes sense to marry a person that's rooting for you, cheering for you, uplifting you, and wants you to succeed.

Pat, who had a heartbreaking divorce from his first wife, Jill, decades ago, applied those lessons to his current wife of twenty-five years, Ruth. He said, "I've learned so many lessons in this second go-around. I feel I'm a much better husband now. You never stop learning in the marriage world."

The ever-consummate learner and teacher, Pat shared with me the many lessons on marriage he has had to learn and implement. He started by saying, "Well, I've learned, first of all, you need to spend time with your lady. You need to listen to her. You need to sit down quietly and let her expand and share what's on her heart. Secondly, you need to let her be her own person. You don't want to be a controlling figure in her life. She is not a slave. She has her own life. She has her own opinions. In our case, Ruth and I, we have some common interests. We have an awful lot of uncommon interests. She lets me do what I like to do and want to do, and I'm the same."

He continued, "At night, for example, I like to read, and she likes to watch movies. So she watches her movies on her TV set, and I'm back in my man cave reading my books. And at 10:15, she wants to go to bed, and we've had a happy evening. And I'm not yelping at her about doing something that she doesn't want to do because I think she should do it. I've learned to encourage my wife to uplift her, to praise her, to do kind things, and to hold her hand—because if I stop holding her hand," he said while laughing, "she goes shopping!" Pat ended his thought by saying, "Those are only some of the things that I've learned, but the key to a happy life is marrying the right person."

Waymakers know the value of help. Waymakers, by nature, are fulfilled when they are able to help others, so it stands to reason that they would also be extremely eager to receive similar guidance if they are on a trail that is causing them difficulty. For many of us, God created a spouse as the ultimate help in life. In Genesis 2:18, one of the first scriptures in the Bible, God describes this need by saying, "It is not good for the man to be alone. I will make a helper who is just right for him." In addition to good advice from Coach Krzyzewski, Pat learned that marrying the right person is a biblical principle.

Our spouse will often be our greatest helper. Some translations of that same verse from Genesis above replace the word *helper* with *help meet*—a curious term uncommon in today's language outside the Christian church. A help meet, however, is part of an action plan for the life of a waymaker to be successful. As the term implies, a good spouse is there to help meet goals—something found in abundance in the Williams household.

Find a Good Thing

Pat's new wife, Ruth, inherited eighteen of Pat's children to help raise. In addition, Ruth, who is sometimes called "Saint Ruth," brought her only biological daughter, Stephanie, into the family to increase the final tally of children in the house to nineteen. Previously an only child, Stephanie always wanted to have brothers and sisters. Pat once jokingly asked her after joining the family, "Do you think you have enough siblings now?"

There are those who have wondered how Ruth was able to take on her new role as mom. Ruth, however, was confident in her ability to be the right wife and mother for Pat and his children. She said, "I knew it would be challenging, but I also knew that I could be a big blessing. I kind of relished the thought of being able to come and bring them love, concern, and camaraderie."

Ruth was first introduced to Pat at an Orlando Magic retreat, where she was a guest speaker representing Franklin Covey. Ruth said that Pat's faith played a necessary role in why the two eventually married. "I met Pat when he offered to walk me to my car. It was very important to me that I found a man who was very deep into his faith. At the very beginning, after reading one of Pat's books that he gave me the night we met and just from speaking with him, I knew that he was that person."

Once married, faith continued to play a major role in how Pat and Ruth parented their children, navigated Pat's cancer diagnosis, and treated one another. A great example of their great faith-fueled love for one another was displayed while the couple was locked down in their home—along with every other American during the COVID-19 shutdown that occurred during the first half of 2020. Ruth said, "During the coronavirus stay-at-home orders, Pat decided to have a contest to see who could be the kindest.

"We would just do nice things for each other," Ruth said while describing some of the contest results. "He's not supposed to eat a lot of dessert, but because he's been so cooped up, I got a coconut cream pie for him or I'll go get the newspapers for him in the mornings. And he keeps saying, 'Okay, you're beating me.' A key to our marriage is being kind to one another."

Another great way Pat put his waymaker ability to serve others into his marriage is through intentional dating. Ruth said, "He was big on dating. He would make a big deal to the kids, saying, 'Mom and I are going on a date night.' I can remember the kids saying, 'What do you mean *date*? You're married.' Pat would say, 'But you can't stop dating.' I think that was key because we had so many things going on—recitals, sports, and all of that."

Ruth continued, "But he carved out the time. And made sure that we dated. I probably would have just kept going with the day-to-day routine—get this done, get that done—because I'm pretty good at organizing. I can be a perfectionist from time to time with that. He would say, 'No, we have to go on a date. Let's go. And we're not going to talk about the kids. We're just going to talk about other stuff.' He is very good about that. I learned you have to keep dating because when the kids leave, then it's just the two of you. And if you don't have kids' activities, you've got to have other things in common."

Pat has run into his share of troubles navigating the marriage road, but he knows the value Ruth brings to his life. Those troubles, it seems, give substantial weight to the lessons Pat shares with others regarding how to maintain a good marriage. "It isn't automatic," he said. "You have to work hard to develop a good marriage. You'll see, though, that the hard work is well worth it." ★

CHAPTER SIXTEEN

FOCUS ON FAMILY

More than a Mentor

"We were the Duggars before the Duggars," Pat's daughter Karyn Williams told me while describing how her life in a house with eighteen siblings compared to the popular show on TLC called *19 Kids and Counting*. "Thank goodness reality TV didn't exist when I was growing up because we would have had our own show. I'm not sure we would have wanted to share all of that. My dad, and the rest of us, have tried to be honest about the fact that it was not easy. We'd be flat-out lying if we said it was."

Karyn, who is Pat's only biological daughter, understands the hard work that went into raising and launching the Williams children. "No part of what my parents did was easy, but it was worth it. And I'll take worth it over easy any day."

Waymakers are often seen helping others succeed in their careers or aspirations. Being a mentor is often rewarding work for the waymaker but isn't encompassing of all their knowledge. Mentors are usually limited in how much they can help any one person by both time and resources. The close proximity and bonding that commonly exists between a parent and their child, however, goes far beyond any average mentor/mentee relationship. Since parents are usually able to spend so much more of their time and resources with and on their children as opposed to a mentee, it stands to reason that one of—if not *the*—most important waymaker roles comes in the form of being a parent.

During Pat's brief stint overseeing the minor-league Orlando Sun Rays team, he would often bring his family to the ballpark. Shereen Kinder was running the day-to-day operations at the park and remembers "all eighteen kids riding in this huge van. His daughter worked with us. His son Bobby was one of our bat boys."

Shereen shared how one day "Karyn answered the phone, and it was the president of the southern league, Jimmy Bragan. She took all his information. When I talked to him later in the day he said, 'I don't know who that lady is, but she was amazing.' That was Karyn Williams, Pat's twelve-year-old daughter. At twelve, she had the finesse of an adult."

Having Pat's family at the ballpark was "great," Shereen said. "They sold programs, ushered, took tickets, whatever was needed. I remember them all coming down to the field to help pull the tarps at night. Pat just wanted them to experience that. He couldn't get all the family involved with the Magic. At the minor-league games, he could."

Parenting is the most "hands-on work" a waymaker will get with someone they are influencing. As a parent, a waymaker gets the opportunity to mold, shape, teach, and train another person for years and with a variety of lessons and applications. This stands in contrast to the short amount of time or limited lessons a teacher may be able to share with a pupil.

Win-Win Scenario

Susan Cox played an instrumental role in the growth of Pat's family. First, as a member of Holt International, Susan was central in matching, facilitating, and placing Pat's adopted children into his family. Second, she encouraged Pat to add someone new to his life at a critical juncture after Pat's divorce. Susan remembers saying to Pat, "You can't take care of this single-handedly all by yourself and in particular because you're basically doing it as a single father.

"He never wavered ever in his devotion to his children," Susan said about Pat's parenting style. "I know some of the kids have not been easy. I guess when you have that big a family, you're bound to have some kids who are going to be more challenging than others. In addition to some challenges within the family, the process to bring some of the children into the family were similarly difficult."

Susan also shared some insights into the adoption journey the Williams family went on, saying, "Pat didn't want to adopt babies. He wanted older kids who, if they didn't get adopted, weren't going to have a family. Every once in a while, Pat would call me and say, 'What countries are out there now where kids need families the most?'"

After his courtship and marriage to Ruth, Pat was no longer steering the parenting ship by himself. Pat discussed the fortunate timing of Ruth's entrance into the family when he said, "Our ship was about to list. It was taking on water, and we were about to capsize when Ruth came along. She got us organized. Took over everything. At that point, we had sixteen teenagers at the same time. You can imagine all their needs. When Ruth came along, not only did she become 'Mom,' but she became a lot of other things."

For Pat, waymaking as a single parent was not a path he enjoyed blazing himself. Instead, he appreciated what Ruth brought to the house, saying, "Not many women could have walked into a house with eighteen children and handled it with poise. She did not get rattled. It was a very beautiful thing to watch. All the kids accepted her. They call her 'Mom.'"

Upon entering the family, Ruth knew how she wanted to approach her new role as a new parent to eighteen kids, saying, "My goal was to help them make transitions through life and to be successful. In raising my own daughter, my goal was to get her out of the nest, not because I didn't love her, but I wanted her to have a happy, successful, independent life. I had the same goals with them. I wanted them to be happy, independent, and fulfilled in everything they do."

> **Discipline and encouragement were among the story lines that could be easily found on an average day in the Williams home.**

In many ways a waymaker herself, Ruth was another strong figure that the Williams children could follow. A common ideal expressed to the children from both Pat and Ruth: "It doesn't matter what you do; just love what you do so that you enjoy doing it every single day."

Raising a small number of children can be adventurous, but raising nineteen of them only leads to that many more adventures. Discipline and encouragement were among the story lines that could be easily found on an average day in the Williams home. While similar in their parenting styles, Ruth did say, "I was more of a consistent disciplinarian. While he certainly disciplined, he also tended to be more forgiving. Pat is the kindest man I've ever known; he would often want to give them another chance."

Grounding was one method of discipline used in the home, but Pat and Ruth saw the need to use it based on the likes and dislikes of the individual. Ruth said, "One of the younger boys was often in trouble, and we would take away his sports video games because that's what he loved to do. On the other hand, his sister would lose her phone privileges." When their son asked Pat and Ruth why they wouldn't take away his phone privileges instead like his sister, they responded by saying, "Because you never talk on the phone."

Ruth's work for Franklin Covey allows her to teach others about their number-one resource, *The 7 Habits of Highly Effective People*. Not only has she taught the material in seminars similar to the one where she met Pat, but Ruth has practiced the lessons of *7 Habits* in her own home, particularly the win-win scenario.

Ruth said, "I would tell my workshop participants that I used the win-win with all my kids growing up. I did not sit them down and say I was going to execute a win-win agreement on their curfew. Instead, I would simply talk through the win-win parts. I'm constantly looking for opportunities for both parent and child to be win-win, even though there will be situations that can't happen because the children could be in a position to hurt themselves or break the law."

Dinnertime was another potential tension point for the family. "There were nineteen kids, with nineteen different thoughts on what tastes good and what doesn't," Ruth said. "I was probably more lenient with that than Pat was. If I knew that there was one kid who just could not stand broccoli, then I would always make sure I had another vegetable option to choose from. I was never one to force kids to eat something they did not want to eat. Now I was, however, one of those who would not allow sweets every single day or before dinner. But in terms of sitting down to dinner, I wanted it to be a pleasant experience and tried not to force somebody to eat something that they really didn't like."

After years of parenting children in the house, Pat and Ruth have now transitioned into empty nesters who parent from far away. "One of the things that I have told all my children who have children is 'You can be their friend when they're an adult, but you need to be a parent when they're little so they can learn how to live life,'" Ruth said before describing other ways her role as mother has changed in recent years. "One of the best parts about life now is that all my children are my friends, and now we do things that friends would do. We can sit and have coffee and talk, go shopping or go to a movie or whatever, because now we're all adults, and we are friends."

Waymaker Jar

As a father, Pat's ripples of impact in the lives of his nineteen children, their families, and their friends are endless. Until recently, I was having a hard time trying to picture and describe exactly how much Pat's waymaking methods have influenced his family. A recent event, video, and subsequent package in my mailbox from Pat changed all that.

On May 3, 2020, Pat Williams turned eighty years old. A large gathering of friends and family was planned for Orlando to celebrate the event. Plane tickets had been purchased by dozens of friends and family members who would happily spend their hard-earned money to fly across the country for the birthday party of their waymaker. Because of the coronavirus and the nationwide lockdown that occurred in the spring of 2020, that event was canceled.

A new plan was put into place. Instead of a party, friends, family, and acquaintances of Pat Williams were encouraged to come to his home in Orlando for a drive-through birthday party. Video of this celebration was captured, and I was given a link to watch. The video contains drone and handheld footage that captures what looks like hundreds of cars and participants who stopped by to say happy birthday to Pat.

In addition to the balloon-adorned cars, constant barrage of honks, and shouts of "Happy birthday, Pat," there were gifts and notes left behind. Participants of the drive-by celebration were encouraged to write down on a strip of paper their thoughts and expressions about what Pat meant to them. The papers would then be gathered together for Pat so that he could pull one out of a jar each day.

Weeks later, a package arrived in my mailbox with the contents of that jar. Pat wanted to share with me the thoughts of others close to him so I could share them with you. Within moments of realizing what I was looking at and reading through some of the comments, it was no longer difficult for me to describe what Pat meant to those closest to him. He was everything.

To truly know a waymaker is to truly know someone special. A waymaker is someone who challenges you to be the best version of yourself and to be the person you have always wanted to be, even if you didn't think you could be. Many of Pat's children, family members, and friends have done just that. They responded with a drive-through celebration for Pat that could have made some recent family trips to the nearby Disney World look lackluster.

The notes and memories provided to Pat will offer him joy and encouragement for the rest of his days. For us as readers, however, those notes can be a siren call to live the life of a waymaker and challenge ourselves to be the best we can be so that we can teach and train others to do the same. Each of us can leave a legacy that will encourage others for generations to come and, for many of us, that waymaking journey begins with parenting our children.

In this final chapter of our "Waymaking 101" section, I want to share with you a few of those messages left for Pat at his birthday celebration:

Brian White—who is the singer/songwriter husband of Pat's daughter Karyn—said, "I remember the first time I saw the 'Pat Williams effect' in action. We took you to a Nashville Sounds game, and the guy in front of us mentioned that he played for the Cincinnati Reds on the 1990 world championship team. For the next six innings, you proceeded to interview him to find out every single thing about him and his career. The funny thing is, we have stayed friends with Keith Brown to this day, all because of you getting to know him that night. You showed me what it means to take an interest in other people and not just ourselves."

Pat's daughter-in-law Mary Lynn said, "I'll always remember our trip to Boston when Bobby ran the Boston Marathon in your place the year you were diagnosed with multiple myeloma. I remember seeing the excitement and pride on your face when Bobby crossed the finish line and watching you two hug after the race."

Adopted daughter Daniella Ayala shared her memories of running 5K races with Pat right by her side. "I can still hear you from the sidelines shouting, 'Go, Dani! Go!' As I was getting closer to the finish line, I could see you standing there holding your newspaper. I'll never forget the sound of your voice and the look on your face when I would win. The next day we would usually go over my results and discuss how I could do better on my next race. Today, I can still hear your voice in the back of my mind when things get tough at work, school, or in life, saying, 'Don't give up, Dani. Keep going!'"

Those short notes tell a much bigger story. If Pat didn't do another thing the rest of his life, it's clear to see what his encouragement and influence has meant to so many. Pat has already lived a full life, but to know Pat, however, is to know he has no intention of slowing down or stopping his progress while he is living on this side of eternity. He hopes to continue fulfilling "another assignment from God" as long as he has breath in his lungs.

As a waymaker, Pat knows his journey is never finished. There is always someone else to call and encourage. Something else to learn and share with others. Some path worth blazing and a way worth making, so others can follow. ★

ADVANCED WAYMAKING

★ ★ ★

CHAPTER SEVENTEEN

GO THE EXTRA MILE

You're Special Just the Way You Are

In section two of *Waymaker*, we will examine the unique traits and behaviors that are forefront in the life of Pat Williams. Unlike section one, these traits may not always be seen in the lives of every waymaker. Like section one of this book, each chapter's title will be a lesson or observation about the traits that make Pat's life so unique. These advanced-waymaking studies will give us insight into how the life of each waymaker is similar in result but varies in execution.

For those of us interested in becoming waymakers, we should use these examples as guides to our own lives. Examining Pat's advanced-waymaking characteristics against our own special and unique gifts, traits, and behaviors may help us consider those parts of our personalities as attributes that can help us build strong relationships as well as useful tools to benefit others.

I want to start our lessons in advanced waymaking by discussing one of Pat's most essential and unique attributes, which is his desire to always go the extra mile. When I talked with Brian Schmitz, a longtime sportswriter for the *Orlando Sentinel* who has covered Pat's three-plus decade career in Florida, he best identified this essential feature, saying, "The thing about Pat is he is always the guy who does more. People jog, but Pat runs marathons. Some people write a book; Pat writes one hundred. He won't make one call; he'll make twenty-five. He won't raise $10,000; he'll raise $1 million. He doesn't have three kids; he has nineteen, and he will do each of those things of the highest order. That's who Pat is."

Ken "Hawk" Harrelson is a former MLB player and was the radio voice for the Chicago White Sox for three-plus decades. Like Pat, Hawk has been involved in efforts to bring baseball to Orlando. He has seen Pat's extra-mile work ethic up close on a number of occasions and is skeptical of anyone trying to keep up with Pat's pace in life.

He said, "For somebody to try and emulate Pat Williams is crazy. From my perspective, I don't know anyone that could. I know a lot of people in my life, and I just don't know anybody that could do what Pat's done. It takes a heck of a man to do what he's done and be successful like he has. He is a unique guy."

Peter Keratosis of *Orlando Magazine* described how Pat was able to go the extra mile in so many different areas of his life, saying, "When people have goals, we tend to focus on the obstacles. Real or imagined. They see what the roadblocks are going to be, and that often paralyzes most people. Pat, however, has an ability to focus only on the goal because obstacles don't seem to exist with him. They don't paralyze him."

Where some of us would see reasons not to do something, Pat sees a challenge to overcome. When others see no way, Pat becomes determined to show them there is. This fortitude to keep going under nearly any circumstance sets Pat's pace at a speed many of us can't keep up with. Thankfully, not all waymakers have to live at this speed in order to thrive. Instead, each waymaker can find the lane that suits them. As long as our effort continues to focus on helping others, waymaking is possible at any speed. For those who desire to be like Pat, however, this section of chapters will help us throttle up as we aim to live life in the waymaking fast lane.

Pat's Trophy Collection

Peter Kerasotis's previous comments about how Pat's sees the world are not the only insights he has shared about Pat Williams. Peter has covered Pat from a variety of different angles inside the pages of *Orlando Magazine*. One of his articles was an award-winning piece about Pat's collection of books and reading habits, which gave Peter a front-row seat to see how Pat goes the extra mile in those areas of his life.

"I went into his high-ceiling home, and he had rows of book-shelves put up professionally by a carpenter to hold his books. He has his own card catalog system. He owns every book he has ever read," Peter said about his first trip to Pat's home to do research and interviews for his article. After taking Peter into his bedroom to show off the hundreds of books he had yet to read, Pat said to him, "These books scream out to me. They want to be the next one to be read."

Pat admits his library and method of card collection is not high tech. Part of this low-tech method of collecting comes from Pat's disinterest in modern technology. In today's world, everyone has a computer on their desk. Not Pat; he never used a computer at work. Pat has read thousands of books, but not one of them was on an electronic reader. "I like the feel of the pages in my hands," he said. "I want to mark them, dog-ear them, and write in the margins. Once you get finished reading it, it's like a trophy, and you put it on your bookcase, and you can always see it."

Pat's library of books, which started with a childhood book about baseball and has since swelled into a catalogable collection of over thirty thousand, is not even the biggest collection in Pat's possession, because Pat is also a devoted collector of stories and quotes. "Over the years, I would think I have collected millions of quotes," Pat said about the most unique item on his going-the-extra-mile list.

Pat described the level of detail and work that goes into keeping such a dense collection, saying, "They are all written on three-by-five cards. Over forty years, I have collected quotes on maybe fifty or sixty different topics. Later, if I want to read something on motivation, inspiration, optimism, thinking right, or any other topic, I can pull it right out of my collection."

Fran Thomas, who for decades has been Pat's typist, has had the herculean task of typing out all Pat's index cards. "His secretary knew how to use a computer but didn't know how to use a typewriter," Fran said about how she ended up working for Pat. "Each month, he sends me envelopes full of quotes he pulled from the newspaper, magazine articles, or books. He later uses these in his speeches, for his radio show, or for the books he writes."

Pat's collection of index cards is neatly arranged and stacked from ceiling to floor in a custom index card cabinet in his home. Along with quotes, Pat uses that collection to store personal memories and stories he references later as material for each new book he writes. There are also thousands of jokes, good for both a good laugh and as fodder for his speeches. During a speaking event in 1976, Pat met a comedy performer named Ken Hussar who worked with Pat to put that collection of jokes to good use.

"We found we had much in common, particularly when it came to collecting good, clean humor," Ken said. "We published two joke books. Our most recent one contains 6,600 clean one-liners from 250 categories." When I asked Pat about the joke book, Pat proudly shared, "We call them the cream of the cream. They are all battle tested from a lectern somewhere. We like to think it's the most complete collection of clean, one-line humor you're ever going to find."

"I loved that he did these books of jokes," said longtime Phillies announcer and color commentator Chris Wheeler. Chris, who is better known by his moniker "Wheels," used one-liners from Pat's books when he spoke at banquets and other events because they were "so clean." Wheels often joked with Pat to "keep cranking that stuff out."

Wheels and Pat have been friends since back in the 1960s when Pat first worked with the 76ers. Of all the great things he has seen Pat do, Wheels said writing books had to be at the top of the list, saying, "The number-one thing I equate with Pat is his books. I wrote one book, and I thought that was the hardest thing I ever did in my life, but he was always churning out books. There's no telling how many he has now."

Barbour Publishing editor Paul Muckley, who worked with Pat to publish 3 of his now 118 books, said Pat's writings have "a good way of speaking to people and their aspirations. His books with us dealt with leadership and personal improvement and came from the Christian perspective. I think Pat has a good way of getting that message out there. He has such an interesting background. He's done so many things and accomplished so many things, but it never really came across as boastful or out of reach. I just think he has a really good common touch."

Former Minnesota Twins GM Terry Ryan shared how Pat's extra-mile mentality existed when Pat became friends with an equipment manager for the Twins baseball team. Terry said, "A lot of times he would ask me about him because he was a character of the game. When he passed away, I sent Pat a message that we lost him."

Pat also sought to seek further wisdom from Terry, and the two passed thoughts on drafting new players. He said, "Pat was interested in what the [MLB] draft was like and asked, 'How do you set up international scouting?'" Similarly interested, Terry would shoot questions back at Pat, like "What does the NBA do to do their due diligence on a draft?" or "How do you set up your scouting department coverage?"

Terry continued to speak candidly about watching Pat navigate life as a fellow sports executive, saying, "I don't know how he does it all, to be honest with you. He's often running and giving speeches. He's got a lot of energy and a sense of humor. We have a lot of mutual friends in baseball. Even though I make my living in baseball, he probably knows more people in this game than I do."

Going the extra mile is the exhibition of how to live as a waymaker. For Pat, he goes the extra mile while collecting quotes, books, and even relationships with people all across the country. He asks questions to people that you may not think to ask. He finds a way to make the right joke or keep humor in the conversation. His bookshelves are filled with more titles than most libraries. When Pat is interested in something, he finds a way to take that passion and push it beyond normal limits.

Whatever gifts or interests God has given you, perhaps you can also find ways of going the extra mile. Your path doesn't always have to be on one lane either. No one would suspect Pat of being the world's foremost researcher of clean one-liners, but when one of his interests collided with his desire to go the extra mile, it left behind substantial evidence of its effectiveness for others to see. ★

CHAPTER EIGHTEEN

PRACTICE THE SEEK-AND-HUG RULE

Ready or Not, Here I Come

Sam Walton, founder of Walmart, created a number of new ways to do business and exemplify leadership. He frequently took trips to Walmart stores across the country to both observe how he could improve his stores and encourage his associates by talking with them. During these trips, Sam created his own ten-foot rule and later made it a part of the Walmart customer service strategy.

According to the Walmart Museum, "Sam Walton encouraged associates to take this pledge: 'I solemnly promise and declare that every customer that comes within 10 feet of me, I will smile, look them in the eye, greet them, and ask if I can help them.'"

Like Walton, Pat Williams is a keen observer who is interested in helping others. Pat, too, it seems, has created and practices his own type of ten-foot rule—which is the practice of 'If I can see you, I will seek you.' Usually, the seek is succeeded by a hug. Pat has no problem chasing down someone he knows to greet them and look them in the eye. Especially if it is an unexpected encounter.

Former Wake Forest athletic director Ron Wellman was walking through the packed United terminal at Chicago's O'Hare airport when he heard someone shout, "Ron!" A few moments later, Ron said, "Pat was jogging over to me, and he gave me the biggest hug. He's just that kind of guy. He makes you feel good whenever you see him. You walk away from the conversation feeling much better than you did before."

Pat, who somehow also found time to closely follow the world of prep sports in addition to all his other interests, would often call Ron to let him know about a potential student athlete he observed that might be a good fit for his alma mater. "I've got another Demon Deacon for you," Pat would say to Ron on his calls.

Ron also said he frequently invited Pat to speak at their school's North Carolina campus. "His first speech was kind of an optional attendance for student athletes and coaches. There may have been seventy-five people there," Ron said before describing what happened next. "The word got out how great of a motivational speaker he was. Every subsequent meeting that he gave to our department that week was packed because of his wonderful ability to speak. And each time he spoke without looking at a note."

Ron is not the only person Pat has had an unexpected encounter with that led to a hug. "I was in New York City to cover the NBA Draft lottery," said Mike Sielski, sports columnist for the *Philadelphia Inquirer*. "I was staying at the Marriott, and I saw Pat coming out of the hotel. We had not seen each other in a long time. He grabbed me, pulled me right in, and gave me this big hug, saying, 'Oh, Michael, it's so good to see you!'"

Earlier in their relationship, Mike was a beneficiary of the friendship currency Pat spends to connect and help others. Mike said, "My professional mentor was a guy named Bill Lyon, who had worked on a book with Pat called *We Owe You One*. Pat wanted to do a book on Jackie Robinson and wanted to work with a younger writer. Bill put him in touch with me. I had never written a book before. We've stayed in relatively close contact since."

Pat and Mike's book *How to Be Like Jackie Robinson* was one in a series of How to Be Like books Pat wrote over the years, which included profiles on Michael Jordan, Walt Disney, John Wooden, and Jesus, to

> Pat is always looking out for someone to connect with, no matter how far the connections are from his hometown.

name a few. The title of this book, *How to Be Like Pat Williams: The Amazing Life of a Waymaker*, is an homage to the title of his popular book series.

Whether it's Sam Walton or Pat Williams, it seems great leaders can find time to greet those close to them. Pat is always looking out for someone to connect with, no matter how far the connections are from his hometown of Orlando, whether he is walking through an airport in Chicago, a hotel in New York, or on a university campus in North Carolina.

Put Your Money Where Your Mouth Is

In addition to being the one seeking advice, waymakers often have opportunities to be sought after by others. Orlando attorney Mikaela Nix, for example, approached Pat after he gave a speech at a leadership conference she attended at the Citrus Club. She said, "I will never forget the moment that I met Pat Williams. He had a presence about him when he entered the room. He turned that room around and made it his own with ease. I don't think I've ever seen anyone command a room like he did."

Mikaela then explained why she approached Pat after his speech, saying, "A lot of young people today think they can kind of do it on their own, and they take stabs at it. I was wise enough to know at the time that you need a mentor. You need someone to help you grow, and you need to harness that energy the proper way for success."

Pat was happy to spend time mentoring Mikaela. "I call him an extreme energy magnet," she said about their time together. "We had lunch on a quarterly basis. He was almost like my own little board [of directors]. I would have questions about my law firm, and he would work it out with me. He would play devil's advocate with me. Sometimes, he would win. It was just great."

For nearly a decade, Pat encouraged and supported Mikaela as she climbed the ladder from lawyer toward something higher. "On my high pivotal moments, such as when I was appointed to the Charter Review Board of Governors, he was right there. When I was running for state representative, he let me use his name and came to my events. He was always putting his money where his mouth was. He didn't just say he would support you; he was there."

Currently Mikaela is a circuit judge. She said, "I look at myself now, the first African American elected to this position. Pat was right there. Staking yard signs for me, writing letters, keeping me organized, and reminding me to keep God first."

Strangers are not the only types of people who desire to build a closer relationship with Pat. Willa Williams is friends with Pat's daughter Caroline. While they share a last name, they are unrelated.

Because of that similarity, however, Willa has said, "I'm like Pat's twentieth adopted child." She is not alone in this opinion either. Dozens of people I have spoken with for this book have shared the same sentiment. The fact that so many people seem to share that belief and see Pat as a father figure speaks to his incredible relationship skills.

Having twelve brothers and sisters, Willa came from a big family as well. She spent a lot of time with Pat's family and talked about how Pat was able to give her helpful advice as she grew up. She said, "I was a big personality. Life is so hard when you're younger and trying to figure out how to be the same person around everyone because so many people can have a different influence in your life. You want to remain who you are and not change, right? He helped me to be stable and grounded because every time I saw him, he treated me the same. He helped me to stay Willa."

The seek-and-hug rule is simply the desire to get close to those you can learn from or whose friendship you value. Closeness can be a neglected tool in the waymaker arsenal. Some waymakers may think that giving speeches to a crowd is the best way to show themselves a leader. Being able to create, maintain, and build onto one-on-one relationships is where the true skill in leadership is forged.

Pat is no stranger to this behavior himself, having been the one approaching someone he looked up to in order to get closer to someone important to him. Former college and professional basketball coach Jim Lynam said, "I was scouting Wake Forest, and Pat was doing the play-by-play. He recognized me and knew who I was. I didn't know him. He introduced himself and asked me if I would go on the radio with him at halftime."

Pat and Jim continued to cross paths many times over the years because of their involvement in the NBA, especially after Jim's good friend Matt Guokas became the head coach of the 76ers. Their interactions, however, were not limited to time on the court. Jim said, "I have a place in Ocean City, New Jersey. He came to speak at a non-denominational church. It gets a big Sunday crowd, and he literally sold it out twice on the same day. He was phenomenal. He's one of the best 'people persons' I've ever met."

Pat is such a great people person because he genuinely desires to connect with others. Waymakers know the importance of building and maintaining many genuine relationships. While the seek-and-hug rule is not a make-or-break lesson in waymaking, it is still an advance study of how Pat has built his waymaking empire over the years. These little moments make a lasting memory in the lives of those Pat knows. ★

★ ★ ★

CHAPTER NINETEEN

ANSWER YOUR PHONE

Ask, Seek, Knock, Find

"I have never met Pat. I have seen him interviewed on TBN and the 700 Club. I've listened to him a number of times on James Dobson's old program." This was how my conversation with Dean Crowder III started. Dean's story had first been told to me by one of Pat's friends, and I found it to be remarkable. A couple of weeks later, I was able to get in touch with Dean and hear his story firsthand.

"I read his book *Rekindled* at a crucial time in my life," Dean said. "Pat was very transparent about all the problems he had with his wife in the midst of his career path. I was at a time in my life where I was going through similar problems in my marriage. I had gone through the usual route most Christians do—speaking to your pastor and reaching out to close friends. While I was reading the book, I paused and thought, 'I wish I could speak to this guy.'"

In a preinternet world, Dean boldly hunted for a way to reach Pat directly, and eventually he was able to get ahold of his secretary. "I poured my heart out to her," Dean said. "I told her I would really like to talk to Pat. A couple of hours later, Pat called me from his 1980s car phone. I told him everything that was going on in my life and how I identified with both his book and his walk with the Lord."

"Dean." Pat finally responded to the weakened cries of this stranger. "All of the answers that you cannot control at this point in your life, God can." Pat's simple response drew an instantly profound realization for Dean. He said, "This was one of those moments in life that you set apart in your walk. Those things that are really impactful. Those God-wink moments that you never forget." Dean continued, "Pat cut right to the chase. He took my focus away from my terrible situation—which everyone else I had reached out to had tried to do—but he was the one that God appointed to turn my focus upward to the Lord.

"I had three boys, and my ex-wife had left. I was doing huge amounts of ministry work at the time, and nothing made sense. I questioned God: 'Why is this happening to me?' Pat took my perspective off of those internalizing thoughts and put it on Jesus," Dean said before sharing the importance of Pat returning his call. "A five-minute phone call to a guy that was really in need. Those are the things that advance the kingdom. He is one of God's ambassadors."

Pat's single conversation with Dean is one in a number of similar calls Pat has taken. Over the years, a countless number of people have reached out to ask for help in some way. Some of those who reach out could be considered "weird" or have "ulterior motives," as Pat's assistant Andrew Herdliska told me. Andrew also said, "Pat gives everyone the benefit of the doubt. He tries to help them in good faith the first time."

The Magic's chief people officer Audra Romao, who first encountered Pat making copies for his index cards in a company office during her first day in human resources two decades ago, has seen Pat bombarded with requests of all kinds. She said, "He does what Disney calls 'the extra inch.' Instead of just doing enough, Pat does enough to really make somebody feel like they're being heard and give them an extra push they need."

She continued, "He gave so many people so much hope. Even when I would go to lunch with him, people would come up to the table that he didn't even know and say, 'Oh my gosh, I just can't thank you enough. You took my call twenty years ago and said exactly what I needed to hear that day. I'm still working for the same company that you gave me the courage to reach out to.'"

Audra has noticed that "Many people have shared that they would call or write him a note, and he would either pick up the phone or call them right back. Or if they wrote him a letter, he would spend twenty minutes talking to somebody that he didn't know to give them advice. There're so many stories like that. He just has an unbelievable way of bringing people together through his connections."

As a waymaker, helping others is in Pat's DNA. How we help others is dependent upon our gifts, talents, and resources. Pat's opportunity to help more people may be greater than that of someone without his résumé of success, but how Pat selects whom he helps could be the same for all of us, because Pat helps anyone who asks.

Contact Information

Not one to sit in an ivory tower as a successful executive, Pat has made his contact information easily accessible for people. For most of us, a short trip to the local bookstore to find the back page of one of his books will give us all the information we need to find him, a practice he learned from two of his mentors, Bill Veeck and UCLA basketball coach John Wooden.

"Coach Wooden's number was in the phone book," Pat said about his mentor. "If a high school coach wanted to fly to Los Angeles to meet with him, he would spend the day with them. When I get calls or letters from people who want to come and see me, I remind myself, 'Coach did it. Bill Veeck did it. Don't be selfish. Be available.'"

WNBA-player-turned-general-manager Tamika Catchings is another name in a long list of people who sought out Pat for advice only to find a lifelong mentor, life coach, and friend. "It was toward the end of my WNBA career, and I was into a lot of leadership books," Tamika said. After reading one of Pat's books, she was drawn to Pat's contact information in the back pages and said, "I sent him an email, and he remembered who I was because my father played in the NBA."

Tamika had recently moved to Florida; Pat invited her to make the two-hour drive from Tampa Bay and meet him for lunch in Orlando. The invitation was reminiscent of Pat's drive and lunch with Bill Veeck years earlier. She shared the story of their first face-to-face meeting, saying, "When we met in the restaurant, we were there for about two hours. He gave me a stack of books and said, 'You need to read these books. When you think about leadership, these are the books.'"

When Pat tells someone that he or she needs to do something, it is not done in a commanding way. Instead, these firm encouragements are Pat's way of making sure the person on the receiving end of the instruction realizes the extreme importance of the advice, which he has carefully been able to draft through years of learned behavior and personal experience.

Waymakers do not want to waste time handing out advice if the hearer doesn't apply it. A fast way to lose a waymaker mentor is to continually disregard or put off applying a lesson they have taught you. Thankfully, Pat has a way of sharing these instructions with love and concern that makes the hearer want to quickly apply the instruction to their lives. That finesse is a hallmark characteristic of a waymaker.

Bill Veeck, too, had a philosophy to answer his own mail and return all his calls, which is something Pat has practiced ever since he started his career. Pat once received a letter from a young basketball fan named Adam Witty who had read Pat's book *Making Magic*. "I told him I read and liked the book and asked him a couple of questions that came up as I was reading," Adam said about the letter's content. Adam was soon shocked when he not only received a response from Pat but also a basketball signed by Orlando Magic players.

Adam offered to take Pat to lunch and continued his correspondence with him through his college years at Clemson University. At one of their lunches, Pat said, "Adam, you need to start a publishing company." After telling Pat he wasn't sure if he could do it, Adam remembers Pat saying, "Whether you think you can or you can't, you're right." Pat encouraged Adam to be the Sherpa who helps entrepreneurs and business owners become the author of books. Adam eventually started that company, which, fifteen years later, is one of the largest independent business book publishers in the country and the official book publishing imprint of *Forbes* magazine.

By answering his mail and returning phone calls, Pat has been directly or indirectly involved with political appointments, successful business launches, and helping others find new career paths. He has counseled the sick and hurting to look toward Jesus. Pat has even been part of helping people meet their spouse and subsequently starting their families. All this is because he bucks conventional trends of celebrities, executives, and leaders who have gatekeepers that prevent them from talking to anyone unknown. Another case in point is the story of Alabama's secretary of state, John Merrill.

"I was the spokesperson for our school system when I met Pat," John said about his official introduction to his waymaker. A longtime fan of the Philadelphia 76ers team and their championship run in 1983, young John knew who Pat was but had no idea that a future meeting with Pat would help transform his path in life. John read one of Pat's books and, through the contact information on the last page, emailed Pat, letting him know the positive influence and his work in the NBA has had on his life. Pat replied with a nice email and an encouraging follow-up voice mail John kept for a long time.

Pat has begun many relationships with others in the same way he did with John Merrill. This book you are reading is a direct result of a relationship that occurred after a strikingly similar letter I sent to Pat more than five years ago. Similarly, Pat's correspondence with those who reach out to him usually leads others to achieve more in life. Seeing something special in Merrill, Pat told him he should run for public office. Pat said, "You have all the characteristics that we need in a strong leader. I know you've done a good job in the education system, but you really need to consider this."

"He would send me books and sign them to the future governor of Alabama or future president," John went on to say about the encouragement that eventually led him to run for office in Alabama. "I ran for secretary of state in 2014 and was elected, and reelected in 2018, with the largest vote total in the history of the state for any office."

When asked what it felt like to have Pat act as such a strong supporter in his life, John said, "It's so gratifying to know that someone of Pat's stature could have an influence on my life and my family's life simply because he chose to. He didn't have to respond to my email, and he didn't have to call me back. He didn't have to send books. Pat is an individual of excellence because he has chosen to encourage other people. I think people who know Pat grow to achieve more in life because he takes the time to invest in those people's lives even when he doesn't have to."

In addition to offering advice and encouragement to those who come knocking on his door, Pat has offered job opportunities. Josh Looney was a finance major who wanted to work in sports. He said, "I didn't know where, I just wanted a chance. I blindly threw a résumé out to the Magic. Pat called me back a day before I graduated in December, and he offered me a job."

One day, Josh asked Pat why he hired him without any experience in sports. Pat answered, "I wanted someone that was involved." Josh's résumé listed his summer training with the football program in Topeka, as well as his jobs as a sandwich artist, an umpire, and a mailroom clerk. "I didn't have work skills, but I had volunteered for everything on campus."

Today, Josh is the athletic director at Missouri Western State University, and he credits Pat with guiding his path there. "He helped me land a PR spot with the Chiefs when that opened up. I was able to rise through the ranks and pivot into college sports." He also shares with his students the lesson he learned from Pat taking his call. "I tell this story to my athletes all the time. I tell them to give back and keep track of what you are doing because there are people out there that see its value."

As a waymaker, doing whatever we can to help others is what God wants of us. In Hebrews 13:16, the Bible says, "Do not neglect to do good and share what you have, for such sacrifices are pleasing to God." There is no doubt that it is a sacrifice for Pat to answer all his calls and letters, but he has never neglected to do good and share what he has with those who reach out to him. Therefore, when we similarly sacrifice to help whoever asks us, regardless of our position, our sacrifices will be pleasing to God. ★

CHAPTER TWENTY

CONNECT TALENT WITH NEEDS

Look Past the Resume

During the day, John Gabriel worked landscaping jobs in New Jersey. At night, he worked at the Atlantic City racetrack making their promotional videos that ran during simulcasts. His friend John Nash had recently been hired by the Philadelphia 76ers to work under then–general manager Pat Williams. John was looking to follow in his friend's NBA footsteps, and at Nash's behest, John began calling Pat from a pay phone at the Somers Point diner during his landscaping lunch breaks to ask Pat for a job opportunity in pro sports.

"Eventually," John said, "I interviewed with Pat, and he gave me a nice job in the box office selling group tickets." After three weeks in sales, John got a phone call from Pat's administrative assistant asking him to meet Pat and members of the local TV station WPHL at a nearby French restaurant. When John arrived, he was nervous and unsure about what was going on.

Pat looked at Joel, who was the director in charge of production at the station, and said, "Go ahead. Tell him." "We saw your demo reel from the racetrack," Joel said. "It's crazy, but you must have some talent." Pat added, "John, we want you to write and produce our team commercials." A stunned John accepted the new position. He continued to work hard and learn on the job and was later promoted to director of scouting.

When Pat moved to Orlando to found the Magic in 1986, John Gabriel was his first call for help. "I think he needed somebody who could do a little bit of everything," John said about being asked to move to Florida to become the first personnel hire Pat made. "Over the next two years, I got to help pick the colors and the mascot, find the coach, find a practice facility, design the floor and the sky boxes. I was part of a small team that was intricately involved with every aspect of putting the team together."

Along with a lot of guidance from Pat, John moved up the ladder of positions in Orlando. First, he was director of player personnel, then assistant general manager, and after Pat's departure from the role, John succeeded him as general manager of the team. John Gabriel went from cutting lawns in New Jersey to managing an NBA team in Florida because he was bold enough to ask a waymaker for a shot.

Pat's incredible ability to measure talent gave John room to grow into various positions. With a talent honed over time through intentional listening and observation, Pat can clearly identify the right role a person should be in. Waymakers connect people with other people, but really what they do is connect talents with needs. One of

Pat's greatest strengths is being able to have limited familiarity with someone while also leading that person toward the right opportunity for their life.

John Gabriel may not have looked like the right person at the right time to everyone else, but waymakers seem to have an instinctual talent to realize the potential of a person before they have fulfilled it. As a recipient of Pat's waymaking opportunities, John has intentionally kept his door open for others as well, saying, "I've never not returned a phone call or picked up a voice mail and call someone back, because that may be an opportunity for them just the way I got a chance. At the Somers Point diner, the phone's gone, but the memories live on."

One of the beneficiaries of John Gabriel's pay-it-forward mentality was Steve Giles. Steve, who was also a huge fan of the Pat-run Philadelphia 76ers teams, was drawn into pro sports work because of Pat. Steve said, "I was as interested in the construction of the things Pat did building the 76ers teams as I was with the games themselves. Quite frankly, it had a lot to do with why I ended up working in sports."

Years later, John and Steve had a chance encounter that helped put Steve on a new path. Steve said, "While I was a grad student, I was coaching at Georgia Southern, and our team was putting on a tournament. John was there scouting Doug Christie. After the game, I went over and introduced myself to him." Steve had recognized John, both because he had briefly been to Orlando to do graduate course work with the Magic marketing department and as a colleague of Pat, whose career Steve had continued to follow after he left the Sixers.

Steve told John he needed to "do an internship to finish my masters. I would really be interested in doing something on the basketball side." John told Steve, "We actually have an internship where we bring someone your age down and they work in our video room, breaking down film for the coaches and for the drafts. We look for young people like you."

Soon after, the Magic offered Steve a position. He moved to Orlando in April of that same year. A few weeks later, the Magic won the draft lottery that preceded Pat's drafting of Shaquille O'Neal. "Pat's reaction and all the stuff surrounding the lottery are things of lore now at the Magic," Steve added.

For years, Steve had admired and studied Pat's work. He even took a sports marketing course that featured Pat's mentor Bill Veeck. After following Pat for so long, Steve noticed something going underreported about his career, saying, "Pat, in my mind, doesn't get nearly enough recognition. He's in elite company of being someone who's not only been a general manager in basketball but who was also a general manager in baseball. How unheard of is that in the modern sports now? Frankly, it'll probably never happen again."

> "Pat, in my mind, doesn't get nearly enough recognition."

Without knowing it, Pat was able to act as a waymaker for Steve through his work with the 76ers, but it was John Gabriel's desire to pass on opportunities to others that changed Steve's life path. Similar to the opportunity Pat afforded John years earlier, John offered Steve an opportunity, or a path to follow, and that is the real evidence of the lasting impact Pat has had as a waymaker on the world.

Pied Piper Effect

Jeff Ryan started off as an intern for the Orlando Magic. During his early days, he remembers Pat "coming up with promotions like 'toothless night,' where we worked with the local dentist, and they brought dentist chairs out in front of the arena. For every tooth you were missing, we'd give you a free ticket to the game." He added, "Pat had a hat in his office that said, 'Fun is good.' That wasn't just an expression for him, it was his approach to how he went through things."

While Jeff may have started off turning some of Pat's wacky ideas into reality, he eventually found himself at the right place at the right time for Pat to act as a waymaker for him. Jeff said, "I was asked to be an assistant to the chapel program. My job was making sure the locker room was open and the chairs were set up." One day, they needed someone to fill in for the minister. They asked Jeff. He said, "I had never done anything like this. I wasn't looking to be a minister. That wasn't my path. I was terrible."

By the end of the year, however, Jeff was asked to become the permanent team chaplain. He said, "I'm pretty sure they asked the players who they wanted, and they said, 'Jeff, because he was so terrible that he makes us feel really good about our faith.'" He added, "Pat was overseeing that. He was very gracious and encouraging to me."

Jeff wound up filling that role for thirteen seasons. During that time, he said, "I felt God calling me to seminary." He has since transitioned out of sports to pastor a church in Omaha, Nebraska. When he left Orlando, he said, "Pat didn't skip a beat. He gave me a book on Cornhusker coach Tom Osborne. He said, 'You better know who Tom Osborne is if you're going Nebraska.' He also said, 'There's a wonderful Bible scholar named Warren Wiersbe down in Lincoln. Get to know him.' They also gave me a nice framed jersey with my name on it, and Pat was there to present it to me."

On various occasions, Pat has shown a remarkable instinct for helping someone make a way where there seemed to be no path. When he started with the Magic, Jeff Ryan had no plans to go into ministry. Pat saw something in him even he didn't. A waymaker is able to connect talent with needs, even when the talent hasn't fully come to the surface and become recognizable yet.

Another example of when Pat demonstrated this instinct was when Pat met Cari Coats, who was part of the chamber of commerce in Orlando when Pat first came to town in 1986. Pat sensed her talents and invited her to come work with him for the Magic. "I don't know anything about basketball, Pat. I've never even been to a game," she told him. Pat said, "It's immaterial that you've never been to an NBA game. Stick with me and one day you will be one of the highest-ranking women in sports." Cari worked in the NBA for the next sixteen years.

When Cari talked to me about the pied piper effect Pat had on her career, she said, "I think everybody needs people like Pat in their lives, to help them see a new reality that maybe they don't see. That was a real crossroads time for me, one of those forks in the road that we all encounter whether we're aware of it or not at the time. When I reflect back on my very successful career, it was because of Pat that I took the left turn and not the right turn."

Sports broadcaster Chip Caray is another example of Pat sizing up the person instead of the résumé. "I was a guy Pat took a chance on when nobody else would have," he said. Chip, who is the grandson of legendary Cubs announcer Harry Caray, was another beneficiary of Pat spending his friendship currency to connect a talent with a need. "I was two years out of college and had very little play-by-play experience." Bob Neil, who worked for TNT and knew Pat from his time with the Chicago Bulls and Atlanta Hawks, passed on Chip's name to Pat when they were looking for a broadcaster for the new team in Orlando.

Pat called Chip, and he later landed the job doing the play-by-play for the Orlando Magic. Chip, however, was not sure that his time would last, saying, "I'm honest enough to tell you that the first year the Magic fielded a team they only won eighteen games, and I was worse than the team! But Pat understood that, and he allowed me the luxury of doing what Bill Veeck probably did for him. And that is to let him grow and learn on the job and learn from your mistakes and your successes and see where that takes you."

Chip overcame those early hurdles to have a successful career in broadcasting. Most recently, he has spent the last decade as the voice of the Atlanta Braves on Fox Sports Southwest. Chip acknowledged how Pat's decision to hire him significantly contributed to his current career and family makeup, adding, "Pat's among the greatest of the great."

In addition to hiring the right person, there are times where Pat's advice for a particular talent is to stay put. Women's head basketball coach Lynn Bria said, "I've been at Stetson University for over twelve years, largely due to Pat. I have had opportunities to leave here, but he's impacted me personally in regards to my faith. It's very hard in this business to find people who believe in Jesus and who aren't afraid to share that."

She continued, "When I had to make hard decisions about whether to stay or leave here because of other opportunities that maybe were more lucrative, Pat helped ground me and bring me back to what's really important. And that's where God wants me." Lynn recalled Pat's response to her the most recent time she brought up a potential career change to him. He said, "Lynn, let me be clear. You're not qualified to do anything else. Stick to coaching because you're great at it. That's what you're supposed to do. It's what God called you to do."

While Pat's advice and encouragement centers mostly around sports and leadership, his reach goes beyond those worlds. When waymaking for Melissa Anschutz, Pat left the basketball arena for the theater. "I work for Baker Publishing Group [as a publicist]," Melissa said. "We've done two books together, including *Character Carved in Stone*. I took who he was and what he wrote in his books and then pitched him with [the] media, and they just ate it up and loved it. We were doing quite a bit of traveling together to the 700 Club and to Nashville for the Mike Huckabee Show."

On those trips, Pat began learning about his new colleague. He then took the time, as he so often does, to engage her about her interests and road map for life. She said, "I came from a film and television background where I was an actress and producer. He was just so fascinated with that. Actually, he had me do a skit right before the 700 Club, just ad-libbing. It was kind of a dramatic scene and I started crying and shaking and did my thing as an actor and stood up and threw my napkin." After her performance, Melissa said Pat applauded her acting chops and told her, "You do not need to be a publicist" and that she should instead "go after that dream."

Melissa initially laughed off the sweet compliments of her new friend, but Pat quickly jumped in, saying, "Don't do that. I mean it, you've got to get out there." Pat put on his waymaker coat to become the person Melissa needed in that moment, which was someone who truly believed in her talents and would encourage her to not stop chasing her passions. Pat then proceeded to discuss what Melissa's next move could be, asking, "What do you need to do? What's your next move?" Later in the day, Melissa saw Pat exercising his friendship currency muscles in person: "He would tell everyone at the 700 Club, 'This is who you need to be interviewing, because she is the star here.'"

Later, Pat picked up where he left off when they reconnected at a National Religious Broadcasters (NRB) convention to promote the book. "He went through the entire NRB, up to every single film booth, and said, 'Have I got the actor for you. I'm telling you it's

Melissa Anschutz. She needs to be in your next film.' He was literally selling me through an area where he's supposed to be selling himself," Melissa said prior to pinpointing how she saw Pat. "This speaks to how completely unselfish the man is. Not only does he encourage you, but he'll promote you and literally try to thrust your career forward if he believes in you."

Promoting the talent of others was commonplace during Pat's travels because waymakers find ways to continually connect talent with needs. Sometimes those needs are his own. While in Orange County, California, at a CBA convention (a Christian book convention), Pat was able to connect with a woman named Peg Rose. Peg was speaking with a man from Philadelphia who noticed Pat across the room and wanted to speak with him. Peg followed.

"My friend knew Pat from the 76ers," Peg said, but she was not entirely unfamiliar with who Pat was. "I read some of his books about Walt Disney. I had worked at Disneyland as a communicator. I was quite interested in his perspective on Walt Disney. So I walked up to him and told Pat I used to work at Disney and had read the books on Walt. He said, 'Oh, I'm getting ready to write another book about Walt. Maybe you could help me.' And it just turned out to be a perfect partnership."

The connection between Pat and Peg was unlikely for a number of reasons, including that they lived on opposite sides of the country, and Peg had only recently left corporate America to become a freelance writer. She said, "I'd waited until pretty late in life to do that, because I was already in my fifties by that time. It's a little hard to get yourself started as a freelance writer at that age, but I've had a really good run thanks to Pat."

Their run began with Peg's contributions to Pat's book *How to Be Like Walt*. Peg noted she "was uniquely positioned to get in contact, to get in close to people, to get the information needed." During the course of that project, Peg also "learned the art of collaborative writing," which came in handy later when Pat tapped her to collaborate on his books *Read For Your Life* and *Lincoln Speaks to Leaders*. Pat also used friendship currency to connect Peg with his daughter Karyn to help with her book, *The Takeaway*.

Working with Pat gave Peg a valuable insight into the way he works and thinks—or perhaps how he never stops thinking. Peg said Pat would call "at any moment, night or day" to give her "gold" thoughts about whatever book they were working on at the time. One time, she said, "I got a call from Pat as he was running the Boston Marathon. He said he was at the top of Heartbreak Hill!"

Never one to miss a moment in life, Pat working on a book while running the Boston Marathon is another example of Pat taking time maximization to new levels, a lesson Peg learned to "always be ready for." Besides being a great teacher, Peg also credits Pat with being a waymaker in her life, saying, "He gave me an opportunity that I wouldn't have had otherwise." Her comment, while simply stated, is a profound expression of the type of life Pat has lived.

Turning Point

Landey Patton was a commercial real estate developer in Chicago during the time Pat was the general manager of the Chicago Bulls. After reading about Pat in the paper, Landey arranged a meeting. Landey said, "I went over and met him and asked how I could help him. I offered to start a fan club, and Pat said, 'I don't need a fan club, but I do need somebody to be a mascot.'"

In the early days of Pat's NBA career, which started in the late 1960s, halftime entertainment, promotional giveaways, dance teams,

T-shirt cannons, and other common staples of today's games were scarce, if they even existed. For this reason, Pat's promotional mind to create ideas, his propensity to try those new ideas, and the bounce-back attitude needed when ideas didn't land, put him in a prime position for success. He found success, in part, because he was willing to do things no one else had done. He has always had a vision to make things better including people, communities, and sports teams.

So when Pat told Landey, 'I want the Bulls to have a mascot,' there was no frame of reference for him to understand what that entailed. Pat said, "Come to the home games, roam around the room, interface with people, and get the crowd excited." Initially, Landey wasn't keen on walking out Pat's idea. Instead, he asked his friends and acquaintances if they would be interested in the job. When no one stepped up, Landey told Pat, "If you think I can do it, I'll be happy to give it a try." He went on to say, "That was all Pat wanted to hear. He basically just wanted a live body that would do it. So I did it. Frankly, it was one of the most fun things I ever did in my life."

Landey's first games were far from the slam dunk spectaculars you see mascots perform at NBA games today. In fact, the bull costume didn't have a name at first. Eventually, Pat named the mascot Benny the Bull after the Chicago Bulls public relations manager, Ben Bentley. During those early years as Benny the Bull, Landey said, "I would be looking for a boy somewhere between eight and ten years old with his dad and mom. I would take him down on the stadium floor where the players were playing. Then I would go up into the stands and shake hands and visit fans. I developed some routines, but I basically just tried to be lovable."

Landey shared one of his routines, saying, "Since I was Benny the Bull, I carried around a sign that said, 'Where's Heidi the Heifer?'" Landey, who wore the Benny the Bull costume for three years, worked for free at first. At some point, he said, "I negotiated a contract for $1,000 a month." The contract also provided him the opportunity to travel with the team. Not only was he the first mascot in the NBA, but he was the first to travel with the team, thus becoming the first mascot many NBA fans who lived in places other than Chicago saw.

Pat's idea to create a mascot for the Bulls created a turning point for the NBA to follow. This one idea didn't just bring a creative element to the games, it helped shift the idea of pro basketball from simply a game to that of world sports entertainment—which some believe now focuses more on the entertainment. Either way. Without these types of ideas, the NBA probably wouldn't be the multibillion-dollar industry it is today.

While Pat was in Chicago, the Bulls were not the hottest ticket in town. Their home court, however, became a perennial sellout when Michael Jordan arrived years later. Phil Johnson, who was an assistant coach with the Bulls while Pat was running the team, said, "The Bulls had a good team, but they weren't the Bears, Black Hawks, Cubs, or White Sox. Pat brought the Bulls publicity. That, coupled with the winning, really helped matters."

Sam Smith covers the Bulls as a sportswriter and is the author of the *New York Times* bestseller *The Jordan Rules*. In an article from 2012 on nba.com, Sam wrote, "Perhaps as much as anyone, Pat Williams saved pro basketball in Chicago. It was in critical condition and facing a sporting last rites when Williams came to the Bulls to play promoter, cheerleader, innovator, and executive. The result was the first great run of pro basketball in Chicago after some half-dozen pro franchises had folded or left the city."

Sam also wrote, "Maybe if there were no Pat Williams, there would not have been six Bulls championships and maybe no Michael Jordan." Without knowing it, Pat made a way for the city of Chicago to receive one of the city's greatest gifts in Jordan. All because Pat had a then-crazy idea to dress someone up like a bull.

The New Normal

Unlike the early days of Benny the Bull, the world of mascots has now become its own professional business. Mascot schools are now open throughout the country, training students to become performers that flip, dance, dunk, and entertain. Mascots are no longer limited to waving at the crowd or walking with a child near the court. Today, mascots are both talented and recruited, with top NBA mascots making six-figure salaries. A far cry from the volunteer work Landey did as a mascot in his first season.

Dave Raymond, who founded Raymond Entertainment, is a leader in the world of professional mascots. He said, "Pat really inspired people to understand how important it is to focus on your presentations and entertainment, as opposed to a game that everyone was emotionally connected to wins or losses, because it just isn't true. The way you build passionate fans that care about wins or losses is to show them how much fun it is to be in your environment."

While you may not know Dave by name, if you have ever seen the Philadelphia Phillies mascot Phillie Phanatic in action, you have likely seen Dave at work. Dave spent twenty-five years performing as the Phanatic and crossed paths with Pat during that tenure. Dave later founded Raymond Entertainment as a one-stop-shop for sports teams and companies looking for mascots, offering design and branding services as well as placement and training for performers.

Dave knows better than most how Pat's pushing the mascot forward in the NBA has created a higher entertainment level than some people understand or give value to. He said, "In Major League

Baseball today, with one broad stroke, they dismiss the mascot and lump the mascot in with clubhouse personnel and other nonessential components. By that broad-brush dismissal, it just demonstrates that they don't see what they have. They look at their mascots as crazy, wacky personalities that jump into a suit and run around and act silly.

"The NBA," Dave went on to say about the differences between the two leagues, "has a whole division in their New York office to highlight game production and to award best practices to mascots and the brands that those mascots are. Pat has always understood their value and invested the time and effort in it. With tremendous passion and excitement, Pat has dug down into the deepest details of building a character brand. And he's somebody that's highly respected and is well versed outside of sports and in life. He values entertainment as being a vital part of building fans."

Not one to let everyone else have all the fun, Pat, too, got in on the mascot action one night before a game against Seattle, saying, "We had a new costume. It wasn't being well received. I thought, 'It can't be that hard.' I wanted to see for myself, so I put on the suit and pranced around all evening. It did give me a whole new perspective. You're hidden behind that costume, and you can do anything you want. I never could dance, but I tried to be as lively as I could."

Pat also recalled a nearly legendary moment that took place while he was with Chicago. "It was my first year there; Dick Motta was the coach. One night he was ejected from the game. I went to the locker room to check on him. Finally, I said, 'Dick, I've got an idea. Why don't you get in the Benny the Bull suit and coach from behind the bench? They'll never know the difference.'"

Coach Motta didn't do it, but "years later," Pat said he heard Dick say, "My greatest regret in my coaching career was that I didn't get in the costume and coach that night. It would've been one for the ages."

Today, Pat still has mascots on the mind as he dreams of the days of professional baseball coming to Orlando. "The ultimate mascot in sports is the famous chicken who has been running around the baseball world for decades. He won't last forever," Pat said in a discussion about what the mascot for the potential Orlando Dreamers team would be.

"We need a mascot that would be that memorable that people would come to the game, in many ways, just to see the mascot. That's how good the chicken is. He fills up ballparks early, and he is a show." For now, Pat has his eyes on a frog for the Dreamers. "I think that's the ticket," he said. "A saucy, impudent yet loving frog. We can call him Kiss the Frog. He'll be out in his lily pond at center field right before the game. A rocket will shoot him across the park and have him land at home plate."

Pat's imagination for promotion and marketing still runs wild at eighty-one years old. He has the ability to see treasure in seemingly unimportant things, even if others can't see it for themselves. If Pat is successful in bringing baseball to Orlando, there will likely be a number of attractions and opportunities for fan enjoyment at the ballpark that no one has ever seen. After all, Pat's promotional gifting hasn't been utilized in the world of baseball since the 1960s. Decades from now, baseball fans in parks across the country may come to experience fun at games in ways that are normal to them but seem unusual or unnecessary to us today. That is how the NBA considered

> **[Pat] has the ability to see treasure in seemingly unimportant things, even if others can't see it for themselves.**

the first mascot. As a waymaker, Pat can guide others to find new ways to enjoy a night at the ballpark in the same way he could help someone in the crowd find the right path in life.

A Place to Stay

Waymakers live to see others thrive in the right roles. Pat loves to see others get promoted. He also isn't afraid to share the limelight or that someone might pass him up on the ladder of success. Instead, Pat is motivated to see talent thrive in the right areas of need. Much of Pat's advice is based on the talent and needs of that person. Sometimes the best advice you'll get from Pat is to stay where you are. Lynn Bria, who was given the advice to stay put in her coaching job, commented, "He tells you the truth, but it also encourages and inspires you to feel like you can do anything."

Pete Delkus met Pat while playing minor-league baseball for the Orlando Sun Rays, which was in the Minnesota Twins farm system in the early '90s. At the time, Pat was dual managing the Sun Rays and the Magic. Pete remembered, "I didn't know anybody. I didn't know where to stay. I met this guy Pat Williams in the clubhouse. He came up to me and said, 'Welcome to the team.'"

After a brief conversation, Pat asked Pete if he had a place to stay. Pete, who came to the team midseason and was making $1,200 a month as a minor-league player, said, "No, and I don't have much money." Pat then offered Pete the opportunity to stay in his guest-house in Orlando. "I'll never forget it," Pete said. Even though they had met only moments ago, Pat again flexed his waymaker muscles to help someone in need.

Pete stayed there through the end of the baseball season and said, "It was just amazing to get to know Pat, because Pat knew everybody. I got to know what a caring, compassionate, smart, crazy-hardworking guy he was. It was pretty cool that I got to live with a guy like this."

The following year, Pete injured himself while at spring training with the Twins organization. "My baseball career was over," Pete said. Facing serious life decisions and looking for advice, Pete called Pat: "I'm in Orlando. The Twins said they can send me back to my hometown of St. Louis for surgery. I can also go to Orlando, or they'll send me to Minnesota. I don't know what to do. Pat said, 'What are you thinking?' I said, 'Well, I've got this television degree.' He goes, 'Why don't you come back to Orlando? The Twins team physician is still here. You could have surgery and rehab here. Why don't you do an internship at one of the TV stations here?'"

Pete thought it was a good idea but didn't know where he would live. Pat again offered Pete his guesthouse. Pete stayed there for another year. Pat and other family members also visited Pete in the hospital when he was recovering from surgery. Pat even called Pete's parents in St. Louis to keep them updated during his surgery. When he recovered, Pat used some of his connections to get Pete an internship at an ABC station in Orlando.

Realizing the value of being in Pat's orbit, Pete tried to make the best of his time with Pat, saying, "I just kept asking Pat for advice." One piece of waymaking advice came after the weatherman at his television station passed away and they were looking for a replacement. "You're going to do it, right?" Pat asked Pete when he shared the news.

Pete was hoping to become a sports broadcaster and told Pat he was reluctant to take the new position because "I don't know anything about the weather." To which Pat jokingly replied, "Well, which one of you weather guys does know something about the weather?" Pat also encouraged Pete by adding, "You should do it. It's an opportunity in the TV business. You've positioned yourself for this."

After a few opportunities to do weather on weekend broadcasts, Pete was offered the Monday–Friday weatherman job, and he accepted. Pete said, "I also went back to school and got a master's degree on Pat's insistence. Now, it's been like twenty-eight years that I've been a meteorologist."

Pete's successful career path allowed him to move out of the guesthouse and eventually took him to an ABC station in Dallas, where he has been for the last fifteen years. While on a book tour a few years ago, Pat was invited to Pete's ABC studios to be a guest on the station's morning show. The station's producer had heard about Pat and Pete's history and invited Pete to come to the station the morning of the live interview.

Pete said, "I'll never forget peeking around the studio, and I could hear Pat's voice. He was talking about his newest book, and they put a mic on me, and I just walked in live on-air and surprised him. We both cried a little bit, you know; we both laughed, and it was just a genuine moment of two people."

Pete said he could still remember the feeling of that day because Pat "has done so much for me in my life. Pat guided me along in those early, extremely formative years, when you need a strong, smart, and, most importantly, wise person to give you advice. Pat Williams was that guy in my life. Thank God, that the good Lord put someone in my life like Pat Williams to guide me along." ★

★ ★ ★

CHAPTER TWENTY-ONE

BECOME A SHOWMAN

Mature in Your Gifts

"Pat was the master of a three-ring circus," said Pat's former 76ers employee Andy Dolich. The carnival barker description he received was in addition to names like "Pied Piper" or "P. T. Barnum" that many others used to describe Pat's effectiveness as a promoter.

"Similar to how an artist might say they learned his or her style from an early impressionists' group on the Left Bank of Paris," Andy said, "I was a member of the Pat Williams School of Promotion. He was smart enough to see what Bill Veeck had done, and he modernized it to a certain extent." Andy went on to speak about the extreme impact Pat's ability to promote well has had during his fifty years in pro sports, saying, "He realistically brought millions, if not tens of millions, into stadiums to see the greatest athletes in the world do their thing in an unscripted setting."

Every waymaker possesses certain unique traits and qualities. Pat's ability to promote has been one of his most successful abilities, while also providing some of Pat's quirkiest stories.

Upon discovery of Bill Veeck's method of success—which was to focus on getting fans to the ballpark instead of worrying about the box score—Pat realized his effectiveness would rely on the ideas he could come up with. In other words, he needed to mature in his promotional gifting. "I would keep thinking deep into the night about promotional ideas or ways to convince people to start attending games and rooting for their team," Pat said about his early years in sports management.

In later years, Pat wrote a book describing some of his experiences in sports marketing, titled *Marketing Your Dreams: Business and Life Lessons from Bill Veeck*. Published by Sports Publishing, the book brought Pat together with their publicist Mike Pearson. Mike said, "He did a series of tours to promote the book. We had spoken any number of times before, but that was actually the very first time that I physically met him."

He added, "Pat was big in the promotion and marketing space. My area was publicity and marketing. We hit it off really well and became good friends. I could call him anytime. Pat is a very affable guy, and it's fun to chat with him, whether there's a reason to chat or not. He's just done so many things." After transitioning into a position as the athletics promotions director at Western Michigan University, Mike found himself borrowing some of Pat's ideas. He said, "So much of it was in the line of Pat Williams. So our promotions kind of fit his personality."

With imitation being the sincerest form of flattery, Mike was not the only team or league to borrow from Pat's promotional ideas. Pat seems unbothered by this. On occasion, Pat has participated in the practice as well, saying, "I always had my eyes and ears open, looking for new ideas. I'm always studying what other teams are doing and studying situations locally that might really lend itself to a catchy promotion."

Developing New Acts

On his journey to develop his God-given gifts and talents, Pat learned mostly by experience. He was never afraid to try a new idea. Over the decades, with shifts in technology and culture, promotions continued to change. These changes allowed Pat to stay sharp as opposed to resting on his laurels. The following stories unlock some of the ideas and challenges Pat faced along the way.

During Pat's early years in the NBA, his ideas helped shape the league. Dick Weiss—who is better known as Hoops—is in the National Sportswriter Hall of Fame and covered the NBA during much of Pat's tenure in Philadelphia. He spoke about how Pat's promotional mind helped change the game. He said, "He was the most innovative GM out there. He always made halftime for the fans. Back then, some of the teams just played the game and that was it. Now, everybody has music, cheerleaders, and bobble dolls, but Pat did things that were way ahead of its time."

When Pat led the Philadelphia 76ers to the championship in 1983, Dick remembers, "They had a huge parade down Broad Street. They went to Veterans Stadium, and Philadelphia really turned out." Dick reflected that the championship celebration in 1983 wasn't far removed from the empty seats that filled arenas prior to Pat's arrival in 1974. He said, "The '83 team had a lot of sellouts, but it used to be a struggle getting people to show up. I remember a playoff game against Milwaukee. Only six thousand people showed up, but thirty-three thousand people were across the street watching the Phillies play."

After years in the league, Pat's track record allowed him to confidently stretch out his ideas to new lengths. Current Orlando Magic executive Chris D'Orso remembers Pat booking halftime shows that included "chimpanzees and an alligator wrestling act." He added, "After the three chimpanzees did their act, they'd come off the court and went outside. I asked where they were, and someone opened the side of some trailer that had a big glass window you could look in. The three chimpanzees were sitting at a table, drinking tea out of glass cups and saucers with one of the people from the act."

In his effort to try out new promotional acts, Pat was not afraid to become part of the show himself. Prior to the launch of the inaugural season of the Magic, *Orlando Sentinel* writer Larry Guest said, "Pat was trying to promote a big Florida rivalry with the Miami Heat. They had a scrimmage game down in Miami, and Pat showed up wearing a wolf's head. People started asking, 'Who is this guy?' But it got some attention, especially from Miami."

Former Orlando Chamber of Commerce president Frank Kruppenbacher remembers joining Pat in the rivalry with Miami, saying, "Pat and I were competitive. Pat made a comment about Miami being a safer place because 'they've run out of victims.' I said, 'The difference between heaven and hell is that Orlando is heaven and Miami is hell,' and that was the quote of the day in the *USA Today* sports section."

Eventually the rivalry was so heated the NBA commissioner called and threatened to disqualify the teams from entering the league if they continued making disparaging comments against one another. Frank believes "those were the seeds that led to the NBA saying, 'Hey, we've got a potential great rivalry here in both cities.'" The league, of course, did eventually expand to include both the Orlando and Miami teams, as well as teams in Charlotte and

Minnesota. The Magic-Heat rivalry was then able to begin in earnest and still continues to this day.

Longtime MLB manager Ron Gardenhire was the manager of the Orlando Sun Rays while Pat was briefly overseeing the team. He had a front row seat to Pat's work. He said, "Good bosses surround themselves with really intelligent people who think outside the zones. He wasn't afraid to try new things or make things happen. He had a lot of people thinking outside the zone of normalcy, and they'd come up with some pretty fun stuff.

"Our uniforms alone. Holy cow," Ron added about the bright-pink uniforms the team wore. "We called them magenta. They were definitely different. They were a spandex material that, as you know, you get a little older and your body's not very good for those kinds of things. My clothes didn't always look great, but my players seemed to like them."

Between alligators, pink uniforms, and empty arenas, Pat has faced never-ending opportunities to develop his gifts.

Between alligators, pink uniforms, and empty arenas, Pat has faced never-ending opportunities to develop his gifts. Sportscaster Eddie Doucette spoke about how challenging those periods of growth must have been for Pat, saying, "Remember, he didn't have the tools and the resources to operate with that these guys have today, starting with the in-arena operations, special ops, and video components. Then, of course, you have social media. Pat had none of that, but he did it his way. He did it through his own footwork and getting on the phone and going out and visiting people in all hours of the day and night and getting players to buy into what he was doing when all they wanted to do was put a ball on the hardwood. Pat would make sure that they did a little more. He was a genius."

Eddie went on to surmise just how effective Pat's matured gift of promotion was when he said, "There are some brilliant marketing people in sports today, but the fact of the matter is—Pat Williams stands at the head of that line. The rest of them are behind him."

Showmanship

In Orlando, one of the great ways Pat was able to push into a new realm of marketing and promotion was when he brought on two professional magicians to perform for Magic fans. Giovanni Livera and Tim Glancy were magicians in Orlando serving the convention market primarily. When Tim, who has since passed away, and his partner, Giovanni, learned that the team had been named *Magic*, they looked at each other and said, "We're going to be the official magicians for the Magic."

The problem was, the team was years away from their first tip-off and the need for any performers. In the meantime, through corporate gigs and word of mouth the pair let others know they were still interested in the job. Eventually, Giovanni said, "The Magic had to introduce their mascot, and we knew it was going to be a dragon."

The pair was hired to create a catchy illusion to reveal Orlando's new mascot to the citizens of central Florida. Giovanni said, "Tim and I came up with this great project called *Catching the Dragon*. They were building the arena at the time, and they had those big cranes and dirt movers out on the land. We had this four-foot giant Easter egg, and we called the media to say, 'The guys digging up the foundation for the arena found this giant egg!' The press came from everywhere. By the time they got there, we had stamped out giant footprints and had a scissor lift raise up a dragon trap way above the street. There was a big explosion. The doors flipped open, and there was Stuff the Magic Dragon."

The stunt allowed Tim and Giovanni to fulfill their vision of becoming the official Magic magicians. During the first home games, the duo did close-up magic in the stands for fans, but Giovanni said, "It wasn't working so well." Taking a page out of the Pat Williams playbook, they thought, "What can we do that hasn't been done?"

The first idea was to put a motorcycle helmet fitted with a basketball hoop on fans in the stands while someone else would shoot nerf balls to try to make baskets. "The fan would become a human basketball target," Giovanni said. "They would cheer, and people couldn't wait to get the ball and win a prize."

Big ideas followed. They had an illusion that brought Pat and others out from inside a giant working speaker. Their biggest idea ever, however, involved T-shirts. Giovani said, "We invented the concept of launching T-shirts." Tim and Giovanni evolved the concept of shooting T-shirts into the crowd out of a cannon.

Giovanni is grateful for the opportunity afforded him by Pat Williams, saying, "Pat, Tim, and I were kindred spirits in the sense that we understood it's a show. Some people thought it was a sport, but we looked at it as show business. That's where we came from, and Pat understands showmanship. It's critical to sports. Without it, you might have sports, but nobody's going to show up."

Promoting Others

Pat's promotional prowess was not limited to half-court. As an author of more than a hundred books, Pat has been interviewed on radio and television shows, attended book signings across the country, visited trade shows, and filmed promotional vignettes. During these events, not only will Pat clearly share with others why his book may bless them, but he will likely use that opportunity to lift up the name of someone else as well.

During promotion for his book on Abraham Lincoln called *Lincoln Speaks to Leaders*, Pat was with the cowriter of the book and professional Lincoln impersonator Gene Griessman. Gene remembers, "We did a promotion of that book together. We did some television appearances in Orlando. We had a joint presentation at a university. We have become good friends." Gene soon learned about one of the friendship currency benefits associated with being a waymaker because Pat often "recommended me to do my Lincoln program." Gene added, "He is warmhearted, and everything about him and his relationship with me has been sincere."

Ten years ago, during a speaking trip to Tuscaloosa, Alabama, Pat was intrigued by the visible name of Bear Bryant—the beloved former football coach of the University of Alabama. The streets, bridges, buildings, and university stadium in town all seemed to literally bear his name. Pat launched a mission to write a book about the legendary figure.

Pat asked his friend, Alabama politician John Merrill, whose story we highlighted in chapter 19, where he could find someone with an in-depth knowledge of Bryant to help him write the book. In an exchange of friendship currency, John game him the name Tommy Ford. At the time, Tommy was the associate athletic director for the University of Alabama.

"I had already written five books on Alabama football," Tommy said about why he was the right choice to write what would become the book *Bear Bryant on Leadership*. Tommy also worked with the AA club, which was the letter winners' group, and had access to every Alabama football player's contact information.

Tommy traveled to meet with Pat, where they planned out the contents of the book. Then they went to work interviewing more than two hundred people. The book was published before Alabama's final game of the season in 2010. "I've never been around somebody so contagious. I mean, you can be down in the dumps, despondent, depressed, and you walk away from a fifteen-minute talk with Pat Williams, and you're ready to rock the world," Tommy said about working with Pat.

One year later, Pat was invited to speak at Gridiron, a Christian men's conference, alongside Lou Holtz and Pat Summerall. That year's event was held in the basketball arena in Tuscaloosa, and Tommy said, "We were going to use that opportunity to sell some of those *Bear Bryant on Leadership* books. Well, we set up a table out in the lobby. Pat and I are there to sell and sign books. Well, I'm more of an introvert. I couldn't sell game programs at a football game. That's just not my personality, but I have never seen someone so in tune to marketing like Pat.

"He stood up on the chair and started yelling across the lobby to the thousands of men at the conference," Tommy continued. "He would be yelling, 'Get your books! *Bear Bryant on Leadership*. The greatest coach ever.' I felt like I was at the circus or the carnival." While Tommy may have been surprised by what he saw from Pat, he was more surprised to see it worked. "He got their attention, and they were lined up. I think we sold six hundred books that day. I've never seen anything like it. It was so natural for him to be the hawker, and it was so unnatural for me to do that."

Later, Pat used his friendship currency with Tommy to meet Rob Wilson—who was to Florida State what Tommy Ford was to Alabama. Pat and Rob wrote the book *Bobby Bowden on Leadership*. Pat has never been at a loss for two things—a new book idea or an opportunity to build a new relationship.

In the world Pat inhabits, it's not uncommon for the idea of the six degrees of separation to be more like the one or two degrees of separation. One example is the friendship between Tommy Ford and Mark Atteberry. Tommy found Mark on Facebook after his men's group at church went through Mark's book *The Samson Syndrome*. After attending some football games together, Tommy learned Mark is currently working on two projects with Pat.

Two friends who live in two different states and work in two different professions have, independently of each other, become involved in writing a book project with Pat Williams. This may seem like a coincidence, but it is the waymaking world of Pat Williams, a world of connections.

In 2003, long before Tommy's men's group read *The Samson Syndrome*, Mark sent a copy of the book to Pat Williams. "It was my first book, and I was not in any way, shape, or form well known or famous. The publisher told me I needed to look for some endorsements for the book. I didn't know any famous people and had no idea who to try to contact. I lived in Kissimmee, which is a suburb of Orlando, and of course Pat at that time was very much a high-profile person in the community. So I boxed my manuscript up and dropped it in the mail to the Orlando Magic offices.

"Three days later, I was at my office, and the phone rang, and it was Pat. He absolutely raved about the book. He told me that it got him in trouble because he got it at the office and started reading it at about three or four o'clock in the afternoon. He said he had 'lost all track of time and was late for dinner that night.' From that day forward, he began championing me to all his friends. He got me endorsements for that book from John Maxwell and Jerry Colangelo and all kinds of people that he was gracious enough to contact and say, 'Hey, you need to read this book.'"

In a story reminiscent of Tommy Ford, Mark said about Pat, "We've ended up at the same book conventions a few times. If he sees me doing a book signing and maybe there's fifteen people in my line, he'll just start waving his arms and attracting attention of people in the concourse, saying, 'Everybody come over here!' He starts drawing a crowd, and then he says, 'This is Mark Atteberry; this is one of the greatest authors you'll ever read. Get in this man's line. You need this book.' And I would go from having maybe ten people in my line to having sixty, just because Pat is out in the concourse waving people over. He's done that several times." ★

★ ★ ★

CHAPTER TWENTY-TWO

LEAVE SOMETHING BEHIND

Leadership Letters

In the top drawer of his desk, Tom Smith keeps a document that lists the seven dimensions of leadership. "It's pretty beat up," he said. "But this piece of paper is huge to me. Not necessarily in what it says, but [the] fact that Pat thought I was important enough to meet and give this to."

Weeks earlier, Pat had a seek-and-hug encounter with Tom in the parking lot of the Amway Arena. "The lot was empty except Pat and me. He was on the phone. I quietly told him I had been fired. He ended his call, gave me a hug, and spent a few minutes praying with me. He didn't say this, but what I felt he was telling me is that 'I know I can't help get your job back, but I can help in other ways.'" They met for lunch a few weeks later, and Tom said Pat gave him great advice in addition to that paper on the seven steps of leadership.

"Pat told me I should take a year off. Your body is tired, mentally and physically." Tom, who had been an athletic trainer for the Magic for the past four years, went on to say, "Pat encouraged me to go meet athletic directors from other sports, and not sit in my house but to use the freedom that came with this opportunity to meet the right people and find out what's next.

"It was wonderful advice," Tom said, "because if I sat at home, my wife and I would complain about how unfair it was that I was fired, and that would do me no good. He knew that I needed to have interactions with others so that pit in my stomach didn't go deeper."

One of Pat's advanced-waymaking techniques is his ability to leave behind something for others, not only advice but tangible items that have the potential to be a blessing in the life of one of his friends. For Tom, it was a document on the seven laws of leadership. For Pat's former assistant Latria Leak—who got married, had her first child, and earned a master's degree while they worked together, it's a hand-written letter in her office from him. Pat wrote in the letter, "I will miss you tremendously and already feel a sense of loss. However, it's time for you to grow and advance. I stand by you all the way."

Signed Copy

Nearly everyone I talked with said that Pat has given them a copy of one or more of his books. Each one was usually signed with a note of encouragement. Jacob Stuart was part of the team that helped Pat fulfill his vision of bringing pro basketball to Orlando. In 1989, Jacob received a book from Pat soon after with the inscription, "To Jacob, I could have never done this without you. I'm grateful. Now let's do it again with baseball." The note foreshadowed Pat's current attempt to bring the Dreamers to town.

Many, if not most, of the books Pat hands out come from the trunk of his car. At any speaking event, social gathering, or meeting where Pat can be found, he is quick to take a friend out to his vehicle and give them one of his books. These trunk books are reloaded constantly, and Pat is always at the ready to deliver one of his trunk book-babies into the arms of a new mother or father.

> **Pat is always at the ready to deliver one of his trunk book-babies into the arms of a new mother or father.**

Orlando Magic chief communications officer Joel Glass was one of many to tell a trunk book story. He shared that the first time he met Pat was "when I heard him speak at the University of Florida where I was an assistant sports information director. I followed him out to the parking lot, and he opened up the trunk of his car, and he had all his books in the trunk, and he gave me one. That was my very first impression."

Joel went on to work for the Magic and with Pat for twenty-five years and said that a book isn't the only thing he's gotten from Pat, saying, "The biggest thing I got from Pat is his energy. Every single day he has enthusiasm for life. His energy is so contagious."

Students are another people group valued on Pat's list to both speak and give signed books to. Student Leadership University (SLU) is an Orlando-based school where Pat regularly teaches during the summer. SLU vice president Brent Crowe says the school is usually for "those that demonstrate leadership potential that needs to be cultivated, young people ready to take their life to the next level. We'll have several hundred students every week. We'll run eight conferences in the summer, and Pat will teach once a week at those."

Pat's lessons at SLU vary, but Brent said Pat's content centers around "cultivating your leadership, maximizing your leadership, and the power and importance of reading." The last twenty minutes of each session with Pat allows the students to "get a book signed or ask questions."

Brent has spent quality time with Pat and is always looking to see what Pat leaves behind in the form of answers to questions. He said, "I interviewed him probably twelve years ago for a book project I was doing. Then I was interviewing him for a podcast three months ago. I asked him a question [on the podcast] that I asked him twelve years prior. I wanted to see if he would give the same answer. The question was this: What's the best piece of advice you've ever been given?"

Brent continued, "He gave the exact answer three months ago that he gave twelve years ago. The advice was 'Don't waste your sufferings.' Pat's been through a couple of valleys, but he's always found a way to redeem those sufferings. I think that's one of the key ideas or principles that kind of bubbles up to the surface in his life of leadership."

During my conversation with Steven Strang, founder and editor of *Charisma* magazine, he told me how he recently came across a signed copy of Pat's book called *Mr. Littlejohn's Secrets to Success* that had been given to him. Published twenty years ago, this book lays out sixteen principles of success. Steven found the book to be so inspiring that he had the principles typed up and framed for placement in his office.

Recently, Steven had Pat on his *Strang Report* podcast to discuss the book in further detail and told Pat, "When I'm around you, I'm around greatness." Steven continued, "I say that having interviewed four US presidents and other important people." Pat and Steven aren't necessarily close, but they have run into one another at various community events in Orlando, where they both live. They once talked about Pat's cancer diagnosis during a chance meeting at a local Cracker Barrel. Moments like that have left Steven with an indelible impression about Pat. He said, "Every time I'm around

Pat, he doesn't make me feel like he is some big hot shot. He makes me feel important."

The GM of the Washington Wizards, Tommy Sheppard, said, "Every time I came to Orlando, Pat gave me some books. They are unbelievable road maps. I grew up on maps. My father would put a map up when we were going somewhere. You spread it out and someone laid out a path for how to get from A to B. That's what I got from Pat's books. You walk the trail of not just being an NBA GM, but you walk the trail of being a leader, a Christian, a good person with a North Star and a compass where you can always find your way."

The Biggest Trophy

Through his books, Pat has left thousands of artifacts in the world meant to encourage the recipient. Some artifacts, however, are one-of-a-kind pieces that will be passed on to those closest to Pat—his family. Perhaps the most valuable of these items is Pat's Bible.

Pat's daughter Karyn talked about the significance of owning her dad's Bible, saying, "It would mean everything to me to have that." From the time she was seven years old, she remembers, "He was sitting at his desk studying his Bible. And he's doing it again today. Oh, and again today. Oh, he does this every day." She has never forgotten the persistence her dad exhibited to search God's word every day.

Today, Karyn knows how the behavior he modeled for her and his family at home presented itself when he was in the world, saying, "In the course of a conversation, Bible verses or concepts flow freely off of his tongue. That's confirmation that God's word is planted deep inside him. He's not trying to impress you with his Bible knowledge. It's just in him. It's an overflow from his heart."

"For fifteen years, I created my own study Bible," Pat said about the dedication that went into its creation. "I had a Bible, and I thought, 'I'm going to find commentaries that I can understand.' I got my fine-point, black-ink Bible marking pen and I'm going verse by verse to have notes—either in between the lines or in the margins, for every one of them."

If you want to sum up what makes Pat a waymaker, consider how Pat Williams would sit at his desk every day for a decade and a half and read his Bible, in addition to various commentaries from Chuck Swindoll, Warren Wiersbe, R. C. Sproul, and others. He would then make a note for every verse that he read.

There are 31,102 verses in the Bible. Many people have never even read the entire Bible. Pat not only read the Bible; he meditated on, researched, and commented on each verse. He also made this effort without the thought of publishing it. Instead, this difficult work was for his own personal benefit, not to mention that his daily Bible and commentary reading was in addition to the time spent perusing other books each day.

As Karyn told me, "My dad has accomplished so much. He has all these cool things. Trophies he got from the Magic. Plaques from this hall of fame and that one. NBA trophies galore." My thoughts were of his personal study Bible—which may arguably be the vital accomplishment of his life. No wonder Karyn later told me, "I want that Bible. I will treasure it the rest of my life."

While Karyn may be alone in the fact that her dad has said she is the one who can have his Bible when he's gone on to eternity, I do not think she is alone in the number of people who would treasure reading its contents. Pat has written a lot of books during his publishing career, but I can't imagine leaving something behind more valuable to us all than a last book called *The Pat Williams Study Bible*. ★

CHAPTER TWENTY-THREE

TRANSFORM YOUR LUNCH

What Can I Get You?

For executives, lunch meetings are commonplace. Waymakers, however, are able to turn common events into life-changing situations. We've already learned how Pat has transformed seemingly normal phone calls, airport terminals, and parking lots into moments where monumental memories can be made. Of all the common places to meet and conduct waymaker business, it seems that the lunch meeting is where Pat's waymaking ability is most proficient.

"After church on Sundays, our family would head to a buffet lunch. They were kind of our thing. Dad would usually go around to each of us and ask questions. He is a big question asker. He is always trying to encourage dialogue and discussion to get your mind working," said Bobby Williams—one of Pat's nineteen children, who also pursued a career in professional baseball like his father. While Pat's stay in baseball was short,

Bobby has worked in the MLB for more than two decades. Currently a scout with the Los Angeles Angels, Bobby is also trying to raise twin boys with some of the same philosophies he learned from his father.

Surrounded by his children during family meals, Pat honed his skills of asking good questions and using God's discernment to share his advice. Pat combined the use of these two skills to encourage his children and others to develop an inner monologue of discernment for themselves, which has been paramount to his success as a waymaker.

While the roots of Pat's lunch-meeting successes may have been planted at those family meals, they certainly weren't limited to them. Host of *American Ninja Warrior* Jenn Brown recalled having a meal with Pat where he hosted a one-player game with her called Would You Rather. She said, "He asked me if I would rather be a reporter for *Thursday Night Football* or a producer for the show. He asked if I would rather be running the network as the president of ESPN or be the mayor of Los Angeles. Every time I chose a profession that I would rather be doing, he would then put it up against something else."

Struck by some of the answers she landed on during Pat's questions, Jenn sees that conversation as a watershed moment in how she's made decisions in her life ever since, saying, "Now, I always make sure that I'm following a path of what I'm passionate about. That meeting with Pat really helped me realize that making a difference and helping people is really important to me."

Jenn was not the first to begin using a new decision-making-method path that Pat helped carve out. According to another one of Pat's sons, Thomas, "Playing Would You Rather was Dad's way of gauging what your passion is at the end of the day." Thomas now lives in Oklahoma and isn't having a meal with his dad as frequently as he once did, but Pat is still sowing seed into his life. Thomas said, "He encourages me about fatherhood, among other things. He's always someone I can turn to for counsel. I trust him to give me good advice. I don't think he gets enough thanks from me as far as what kind of impact he's had on my life, but he certainly has."

After retiring from a local NBC affiliate in Orlando, sportscaster Pat Clarke said, "Pat was among the first people to call me." Soon after, the two Pats met for lunch, where Williams asked Clarke to be the publicist for the launch of the Dreamers baseball team in Orlando. Clarke said, "I agreed to become the publicist and then sat at the restaurant for three hours. We ate, but we also shared stories. I don't pinch myself about it anymore, but I don't lose sight of the fact that I had lunch for three hours with a man who shaped professional sports in central Florida."

Each Meal is Different

In addition to meals being a place for guiding someone into a new future, Pat uses meals as a tool to increase his stake in friendship currency. Baseball historian and former public relations director for the New York Yankees, Marty Appel said Pat would "reach out when he came through New York on an interview or book tour." Marty has known Pat since they met at the baseball winter meetings in the late 1960s, but they have only grown close recently, as Pat made intentional efforts to stoke the fires of that relationship through those lunch and dinner meetings. Marty said, "Our friendship really cemented in the last couple of decades.

"Pat is a great organizer," Marty said before describing what their time together looked like when Pat visited. "He would come to New York and put together dinners with Ernie Accorsi and myself. The three of us—who each worked in a different professional sport—would sit there and talk sports way into the night. I thought it was wonderful that this high-placed, respected man would playfully go through all that trouble to organize an evening like that."

One of Pat's favorite places to eat and have meetings is Cracker Barrel. New York sports broadcaster Ann Liguori talked about one such experience, saying, "I was in Florida and wanted to do an interview. I brought my laptop, microphone, and all my equipment, but it was so noisy that we had to do the interview in the front seat of my car."

Ann was undeterred, however, because "I really value his sports knowledge and insight, his business sense, and I'm inspired by his life and what's he been able to do." Plus, she added, "He's been a dear friend of mine for a couple of decades now. He's not a golfer, but he's come up to my golf tournaments. I have a foundation too. I raise money for cancer research and prevention, and we've honored him at one of the dinners here in the Hamptons."

Mark Murphy, president of the Green Bay Packers, explained what it was like to get some one-on-one time with Pat over a meal, saying, "I felt like I was talking to Yoda. Pat's so wise and has so much experience. He has seen everything and has a way of giving advice in a way that is easy to understand."

Mark went on to share one of the words of advice Pat gave him, saying, "It's better to get rid of someone a year or two sooner than a year or two late." The advice—which could easily be pictured coming out of the mouth of a Jedi master—was helpful to Mark in the various positions he has held in pro sports. Mark said, "As an athletic director to my current position, you want to give people every chance to succeed, but sometimes it just wasn't meant to be. And you're better off cutting your losses."

Eagles VP and general manager Howie Roseman is another NFL executive who has benefited from breaking bread with Pat. "Right before the 2017 season, he came with his sister to have lunch with us in Philadelphia. We ended up winning a championship that year," he said. A few years earlier—during a role change for himself within the Eagles organization—Howie spent time trying to visit with people who were exceptional in their field. His various travels to glean from other leaders in the business and sports world led him to a conversation with Pat at a sports conference in Chicago.

Howie said, "Pat talked to me about the ebbs and flows of life, staying positive, and the things I could do better if I ever had the chance in terms of building a culture." Howie—who referred to Pat as the godfather of front-office executives—has held on to the advice Pat passed along. He even saved a voice mail of positivity Pat left him years ago and listens to it when he needs to be encouraged. "I've learned a lot of lessons from Pat. The things he espouses to his team and his leadership. He is a special guy."

For many of us, lunch is a small part of our day; a time to fuel our body or a chance to take a break from the work day. Pat, however, uses his lunchtime as a waymaking opportunity. Each day offers the potential to share his insights and pass on what he has learned to others. In some cases, Pat uses lunch as a tool to get to know someone or as a time to earn more friendship currency to spend later. Regardless of its purpose, Pat has found a way to make lunch about a lot more than food. ★

CHAPTER TWENTY-FOUR

RUN AS FAST AS YOU CAN

I Just Felt Like Running

In an earlier lesson on how to be like Pat, we discussed how he is prone to going the extra mile in various categories of his life. How instead of having three children, Pat had nineteen. Instead of working for a team, he built one. Instead of reading God's word, he wrote a study Bible. Sometimes going the extra mile is easier to do when you are running faster than everyone else. As a waymaker, Pat has outrun the pace of others many times over—packing the achievements of a dozen men into his eighty-one years.

Pat's desire to keep on running reminds me of a beloved fictional character from the movies, Forrest Gump. Played by Tom Hanks in the Oscar-award-winning best picture of 1995, Gump sits on a park bench sharing the stories of his life—which are set against several real events from our nation's history. The viewer is transported to various points in

Gump's life, including accounts of when he led Bear Bryant's Alabama football team to victory, received a Medal of Honor for his service in the Vietnam War, interacted with multiple presidents, and became wealthy after founding his own Bubba Gump Shrimp Company.

In one part of the film, a young Forrest in leg braces is chased by bullies while his childhood friend Jenny yells, "Run, Forrest. Run!" The braces began to break and fall, showcasing a newfound speed that allowed him to escape. In the late 1970s, Forrest uses his legs to run cross-country marathons that, in true waymaker fashion, inspire others to follow behind him and is said to have helped launch the jogging craze.

The weather was often chilly in Philadelphia, but that didn't stop Pat from running up and down the steps or through the breezeway of the stadium.

Pat has been seen as an innovator in the running world himself. Former Philadelphia 76ers GM John Nash was one of many who said Pat was jogging before anyone knew what it was called. John said, "Pat would be running around the concourse, jogging, and Harold Katz, who was then the owner of the 76ers, would want to speak to him. When he couldn't get in touch with Pat, he would then call me and say, 'Where's Pat?' And I said, 'I think he's running.' Harold would tell me, 'You go get him,' and I would then have to jog around that concourse to try to convince Pat to come in and take the phone call."

The weather was often chilly in Philadelphia, but that didn't stop Pat from running up and down the steps or through the breezeway of the stadium. Nash noticed how the weather affected Pat's wardrobe, saying, "Pat didn't have gloves. He wore sweat socks on his hands as he was running." Decades later in the warmer weather of Florida, Pat could still be seen out on a jog.

Patrick Morley, who is the founder of Man in the Mirror Ministries and the author of a best-selling book by the same name, was one of Pat's neighbors. He said, "Pat lived across the lake from us. I could see his house from mine. Our lake is about a half square mile. So it's like a peanut with three lobes, and it goes between four major roads. I remember Pat being a fitness nut. He used to run many miles around the lake on those roads."

While the pair of Pats were neighbors for years, they actually met when Morley, who was an established member of Orlando's business community, heard Pat was a Christian and wanted to get acquainted with someone whom he called "among a handful of the most gifted promoters, publicity people, and marketers that have ever graced our city."

Morley remembers noticing two things about Pat when they met. First, he said, "There was not a piece of paper anywhere on his desk. He's extremely meticulous." The second was that Pat was "very high energy." The relationship born in the office that day was followed by neighborly meetings. Some of their children even played on the same soccer team growing up. Eventually, that relationship allowed Williams to be a waymaker for an influential national ministry.

Morley said, "I was on the board of directors of Campus Crusade for Christ International, but it's now called Cru. They wanted to move their headquarters out of San Bernardino, California." A list of more than thirty cities was drawn up as potential landing spots for the new headquarters, but "Orlando," Morley added, "was not on the list.

"So I called a meeting," Morley said about the chain of events. "There might have been forty leaders in the room. Pat was there. He agreed to serve with me on a little committee. The purpose of the committee was to have a large gathering of Orlando's leaders, including business, political, religious, and others, to express our interest in having Campus Crusade relocate to Orlando."

Morley said, "We had it at the Metroplex of downtown Orlando, and six hundred leaders came out. Every leader in Orlando was there. Every banker. Every major pastor. You could tell it was a God thing." At one of their meetings, Pat expressed to the group, "We'll get this done for you." Morley explained, "That of course meant getting land, raising funds, and so forth."

While those things were important, perhaps the most influential and therefore waymaking thing Pat did was share the right idea at the right time. Soon after telling Cru founder Dr. William Bright that "they would get this done," Pat said, "And before you know it, you'll be sipping orange juice on your back porch." Morley said that statement was one of the things that "affected Dr. Bright the most," and Pat had "a defining influence on the decision to come."

Due in large part to Pat's effectiveness in waymaking, Orlando was eventually chosen to be the world headquarters for this global ministry. They relocated in 1991. In 1999, the *Orlando Sentinel* reported that Cru moved itself into a "$45 million, 600,000-square-foot headquarters," and the ministry "now has a full-time staff of more than 20,000 employees around the world and an annual income approaching $400 million," with "more than 650,000 trained volunteers and 68 ministries in 181 countries."

Don't Get Left Behind

Running seems to have engrained itself as part of the culture of Pat's life. In fact, running fast was the theme of Pat's first book called *The Gingerbread Man*. Coauthored by Jerry Jenkins in 1974, the book tells Pat's story before the Magic, before the nineteen children, and before his fifty-eight marathons.

Jerry Jenkins, the best-selling author of nearly two hundred other books including the popular Left Behind series, was one of the first to take notice of the way Pat's life was passing others by. While working as a sportswriter for a suburban paper in Chicago, Jerry was called on to write a column about Pat and his role as the GM of the Chicago Bulls. "It was something special to see him become the youngest general manager in the history of pro sports when he joined the Chicago Bulls in 1969," Jerry said about his first impressions of Pat.

The meeting for that article led to a desire in Jenkins to write about Pat's entire life. Pat said the book's title *The Gingerbread Man* referred to "an old nursery rhyme. 'Run, run, run as fast as you can, you can't catch me, I'm the gingerbread man.' He rode across the river on the nose of the fox. The nursery rhyme captured who I was at the time. Running as fast as I could to become successful."

Jerry went on to say, "Pat was known in Christian circles for his vibrant testimony and speaking gift, so when I was managing editor of a Sunday school take-home paper in the early 1970s, I landed an interview with him. I had recently left sportswriting to follow a call to full-time Christian work, but I wanted to keep a foot in the sports world, so such a story was ideal for me."

Even though Pat was in his early thirties, Jerry said, "There was more than enough material for his autobiography, and it was quite a ride. Pat was and always has been a house-afire type of personality, brimming with energy and ideas, seemingly 24-7. What most impressed me, and still does, was his unapologetic eagerness to share his faith in any venue."

A shared faith in God was also at the center of a connection Pat orchestrated between Jerry Jenkins and Vietnam War hero Lieutenant Patrick Cleburne McClary. Lieutenant McClary, or Clebe as he is more commonly known, was seriously injured during the war, losing his left arm and left eye in battle. The recipient of numerous awards including three Purple Hearts, Clebe has a tremendous testimony.

Pat has invited his longtime friend Clebe to share his story at multiple NBA chapel services over the years. In addition to those chapel services, Clebe is a highly sought-after speaker on the circuit. Clebe said, "I was speaking at the baseball all-star game out in Oakland. Pat was there and had a couple of his boys with him. Sitting right next to us was NFL coach John Madden. That's where I asked Pat who helped him write his book *Rekindled.*"

Clebe said, "Pat put me in touch with Jerry. He came down and stayed with us for about a week. It snowed. He interviewed my wife and wrote her book *Commitment to Love.* Pat made all that possible. After Jerry sold eighty million copies of *Left Behind.*" Clebe playfully added, "You can't hire him now, but he was really good to us."

Waymakers connect talent with needs, but in doing so they also give others the opportunity to run as fast as they can. Connecting Jerry with the McClarys helped him run faster toward *Left Behind.* For Clebe and his wife, Deanna, they were able to run faster toward helping others through their testimonies. This is only one example of Pat's friendship currency that Clebe has seen exchanged many times over the years, saying, "You just mention something to Pat, and he'll put you in contact with people that can really help you through your life."

Another one of the connections shared between Pat and Clebe is a friendship with former New York Yankee Bobby Richardson. Bobby played for the Yankees from 1955 until 1966, including three championship teams. Bobby and Pat got to know each other while Pat was the general manager of the Spartanburg Phillies. Bobby's home was in Sumter, South Carolina.

"He had me come up and speak to the ball club and be part of an event he was putting on at the [Spartanburg] ballpark that night. We just hit it off and became friends," Bobby said about the origin of his relationship with Pat. Clebe, who was also living in South Carolina, would host the two men and their wives for evenings at their home. Bobby said, "I was sharing my testimony the night that Clebe and his wife, Deanna, accepted Christ."

Connected by Christ, the three men each ran as fast as they could in various areas of experience. Pat respected Bobby so much that he named his second child after him. Each, however, would use speaking opportunities to share Jesus with others. Bobby and Pat both were asked on several occasions to share their testimonies in front of enormous crowds during some Billy Graham revival events.

Pat said, "My first Billy Graham encounter took place when I was a senior at Wake Forest in the spring of 1962. Billy Graham came to our campus for a two-night crusade. I had a radio sports program that I did every week on the campus station. I was able, with my traveling tape recorder, to arrange an interview with him. We talked about sports and went back to his early days. He loved baseball and wanted to be a baseball player.

"Ten years later," Pat continued, "I was the general manager of the Bulls, and Billy Graham had a crusade he brought to Chicago's McCormick Place. Big setting. Forty thousand seats. I got the call asking me to come share my testimony." Pat spoke twice more at events, including the enormous Carrier Dome in Syracuse, New York, and remembers Billy's "powerful voice, with just the right touch of the South to it."

It's Never too Late

Running isn't the only area in life where Pat runs parallel to the life of Forrest Gump. One of the reasons Forrest Gump's life was so compelling to watch on the big screen was because it seemed so unbelievable that one person could fit all those memorable moments and accomplishments into one life. Watching Pat's life, however, may bring someone to similarly believe that Pat's life seems fictional.

From meeting Billy Graham on campus to being near the stage when Martin Luther King Jr. delivered his famous speech in 1963, Pat seems to be similar to Forrest Gump in the sense that he is always in the right place at the right time. Not only that, but Pat has found the time to excel in sports as a player, broadcaster, and executive while also raising nineteen children, writing well over one hundred books, speaking across the country every week, running four marathons a year, hosting three weekly radio shows, maintaining relationships with a countless number of friends and family, reading five hundred books a year, and teaching a Sunday school class.

Pat Williams's life may seem fictional, but it's not. Like Forrest, Pat has learned to run as fast as he can. Only instead of running from bullies, Pat is chasing after his dreams. While Pat may have benefited from starting his race at an early age, chasing his visions from a young age was not a determining factor in why his life is successful. Instead, that advantage only gave him the time to add more items to his list of achievements.

Another example of Pat's tendency to stay active and youthful regardless of his numerical age is his involvement with the MLB's alumni games. These charitable games are often held in Clearwater, Florida, and provide opportunities for retired MLB players, celebrities, and other notable people to share the field together.

Two-time Olympic softball gold medalist Michele Smith was the pitcher on one of the teams for a handful of years. She said, "Pat would catch me. I would throw the ball pretty hard, but he would always volunteer to come out and catch me and always had a smile on his face. That's why I respected him so much. There were some times I'd throw a rise ball, and his glove would never move, and the ball would go right over his head!"

"'Catching games' is an understatement," said retired MLB player and manager Clint Hurdle. "He would catch every game. There'd be ten games, and they were only three innings, but he would catch thirty innings. The humility of that. Talk about service before self, to catch and befriend people and have a small conversation with every hitter."

Since retiring, Clint—who has admired Pat as an "unrelenting visionary"—now lives a couple of hours away from Pat and has plans to stay close to him. He said, "I finally have come upon a season of life in which I have time to give to Pat. I've never had that before. I believe in being a lifelong learner, and he's paved so many different trails and paths that there is a reason he gets people to buy into the vision. He does it without a hammer. His power tools are his compassion and his heart. I have always tried to keep men in my life like that to continue to learn from."

To become a waymaker, you must see your future as an unwritten list of accomplishments. There is still time to be impactful no matter where you are in life or how old you may be. Clint Hurdle still sees Pat as a potential waymaker for him even after he has retired from multiple roles in professional baseball. Pat is over eighty years old and has plans to spend years trying to launch a Major League Baseball team in Orlando.

The term *over the hill* and the word *retirement* are foreign to Pat and those who strive to be like him. Make those terms foreign to yourself, and use whatever time you have to start running. Break free from the braces that hold you back and run toward your goals or toward the future that God has for you. Either way, run as fast as you can. ★

★ ★ ★

CHAPTER TWENTY-FIVE

EVANGELIZE WITHOUT TALKING

Church is Not Just for Sundays

In February 1978, Pat was approached by Philadelphia 76ers player and fellow Christian Bobby Jones to start a chapel program for their Sunday games. The chapel service—which only had four people at their first meeting—was the first of its kind in the NBA. The service has increased in popularity and has since been adopted by every team in the league, and similar game-day services are now commonplace among all professional sports.

In 1981, Pat decided to go the extra mile and helped launch a chapel service for the NBA All-Star Game. The yearly event is a chance for the players and other guests visiting from out of town to attend a worship service together. The NBA All-Star Chapel Service is a highlight event of the weekend where a prominent speaker is invited. John Maxwell, David Jeremiah, Francis Chan, Norm Sonju,

Erwin Lutzer, and James Dobson are among the men who have led the service.

At the 2019 All-Star Game in Charlotte, North Carolina, Pastor David Chadwick was the featured speaker. "I've always known Pat from a distance because I played basketball at North Carolina. I followed his career with the 76ers and the Magic. I didn't get a chance to know him until he invited me to speak at the NBA All-Star Game. That's when we got to spend a lot of time together and just talk and get to know one another," David said.

During their first conversations, basketball was the main focus. Pat dug into David on the subject of the longtime Tar Heel basketball coach Dean Smith. David said, "I wrote a book about Coach Smith about fifteen years ago entitled *It's How You Play the Game: The 12 Leadership Principles of Dean Smith*. Pat wanted to know a lot about Coach Smith. Who he was and how to learn from his leadership because Pat's a real student of leadership."

David also said, "Pat gave me insights into who was probably going to be at the chapel service—folks like Kevin Johnson and David Robinson. He said, 'Here are the things they love to hear about that will encourage them.' So he gave me some talking points that really were helpful, but he really left that up to me, saying, 'You go where the Lord leads you.'"

David also shares a connection with Bobby Jones, who first approached Pat with the idea for regular chapel services. Bobby was a freshman at North Carolina when David was a senior. David laughingly said, "Freshmen were ineligible to play during that time period. So I have always prayed a thanksgiving prayer to God that Bobby wasn't born a year earlier because I would've never played a minute. He was that good."

While Bobby Jones's talent on the court may have gotten him elected into the NBA Hall of Fame, his heart to serve Christ and others may be where his star shines brightest. David used his time with Pat to confirm a story he had heard years prior about Bobby visiting Pat in the hospital on a trip through Charlotte, North Carolina, where Pat had gotten sick.

"Bobby found out about me being ill," Pat said to David, "and I couldn't believe it. One time, I woke up from being heavily medicated, and there was Bobby next to my bedside, changing my bed pans and caring for me like nobody else had. I was sitting there thinking, 'I've got these nurses caring for me, the doctors, of course, but here is an NBA All-Star, now in the Hall of Fame, one of the greatest players who's ever played the game, sitting by my bedside.'"

David said he has often thought of this story as "an example of who Jesus is, the true servant leader, who comes down off the throne to wash the disciple's feet and care for them in the most intimate way. Bobby really gave me a new insight into what true servanthood looks like."

Not one to boast about his service of others, Bobby said about the event, "Pat asked me to come, and I went to see him several times and tried to help him as best I could. He was in intensive care for a bit. That was just a good time of being close to him and to help a friend in a time of need. The lifestyle he has lived gives weight to his life. So when somebody like that asks you for something or asks you to do something, you want to help them because you trust what they're doing in their life is of value. It was really an honor for me to help him."

Both men have been rooted in Christ for years. Bobby said he has continually seen Pat "live his faith. He doesn't wear it on his sleeve, but he is bold in wanting to share Christ with other people. In the arena of the NBA, people look at Christianity as a crutch or a phony thing. Pat lived it authentically over these last fifty years. You can say you don't believe, but here's an example of a guy who gives, has been blessed, and has lived an exemplary life through the Lord."

Track star and friend Monica Cabbler made special efforts to attend the NBA All-Star Chapel Service the year it was held in New Orleans, saying, "I caught a red-eye out Saturday night just to support Pat's chapel service Sunday morning. The next thing I know I am sitting at the NBA Legends brunch with Pat and his family."

Always with his eye out for an opportunity to be someone's waymaker, Monica said, "Pat knew I was looking for a partner with NBA Cares and some of the local LA teams for my foundation, a nonprofit for kids. He gave me the chance to cross paths with newly appointed deputy commissioner of the NBA Mark Tatum and give him a hand-written letter."

> Pat said, "Some of the fellas stepped up and said, 'We feel that Pat Williams should be in charge of this.' I kind of melted down."

In 2011, pastor, leadership expert, and best-selling author John Maxwell was asked by his friend Pat Williams to speak at the all-star service in Washington. After his message that day, Pat told John, "You should share these thoughts with more people by putting them in a book." John did just that. The message became the subject of his book *Running with Giants*. In the first chapter of that book, Maxwell writes, "I took Pat's advice because I want you to be encouraged by the giants of faith, just as I have been."

Arguably a giant of faith himself, Pat has spent his Christian life trying to advance the claims of Christ, first in Spartanburg, where he wanted to bring a chapter of the Fellowship of Christian Athletes (FCA). The vision of the FCA is to see the world transformed by Jesus Christ through the influence of coaches and athletes.

While attending his first meeting on the subject of bringing FCA to Spartanburg, Pat said, "Some of the fellas stepped up and said, 'We feel that Pat Williams should be in charge of this.' I kind of melted down. Really? I'm going to be in charge of bringing the FCA to Spartanburg. That's a pretty big deal. I remember trying to say, 'I don't think so. I'm not qualified. I'm pretty new to this game.'

"Well, they didn't want to hear that," Pat continued on. "They put the thumb on me, and off I went. I remember putting together a banquet. We brought up one of the top executives from the national FCA office to be the speaker. We had this room for a dinner, and it was just packed. It was a very memorable evening."

The Stuff of Legend

Longtime play-by-play announcer for the Minnesota Twins baseball team John Gordon was a classmate and fellow broadcaster with Pat at Indiana University. John was one of the first people Pat was able to act as a waymaker for. "They needed a broadcaster in Spartanburg, South Carolina. Pat called me. I wanted a career in sports broadcasting but not necessarily baseball. But when the opportunity for baseball came up, I just jumped at it."

John remembered being a part of those first FCA meetings. "We had a lot of guys who were active. It was very strong. I remember the luncheons and the big banquet with Dallas Cowboys coach Tom Landry. Pat brought in some outstanding Christians to speak."

In addition to going to school, working for the Spartanburg Phillies, and being a part of the FCA with Pat, John shares another similarity with Pat—they were saved on the same day. According to Spartanburg native Chuck Wallington, who also owns the largest independent Christian bookstore in the country, Pat and John were "iconic in the town." He said, "Spartanburg is a spiritually based small southern town. So the testimony of those two guys getting saved in the same day moved the needle spiritually for everybody."

After leaving baseball in Spartanburg, Pat moved into basketball, where he used his initial FCA experience to launch a chapter of the FCA in Philadelphia during his first year there. He launched another chapter in Chicago during his four years as the GM there. When he came to Orlando, his office happened to be in the same building as the FCA office, and he has worked closely with them ever since.

Longtime senior executive of the Chicago Bears Patrick McCaskey was part of the FCA with Pat. He talked about the importance of Pat's involvement: "I admired him. He was a good athlete and excellent sports executive for fifty years. He had credibility."

As a credible leader, Pat has come a long way from when he was a new believer suddenly thrown into FCA leadership in Spartanburg. He also knows the impact of that first opportunity, saying, "That organization has been a big part of my life. I just keep coming back to the fact that when you surrender your life to God, you better be ready to duck, because things are going to start happening."

The creation of God, Family and Country Night is arguably one of Pat's farthest-reaching and most popular sports promotions. The promotion, however, may also be Pat's greatest evangelistic tool. Pat recalled the origin of the idea, saying, "In 1981, the 76ers were bought by a local businessman named Harold Katz. We were brainstorming about what we could do to increase our attendance. I suggested God, Family and Country Night."

"Good idea," said Harold, who is Jewish. He joked that if they do that, he should run a "God and Country Club Night." Jokes aside, the challenge was on. Harold would have a Jewish night and Pat would have a Christian night, to see which promotion drew better.

"Well, we put it together," Pat said about that first event, and "filled the Spectrum."

Pat continued to describe the details of the event. "After the game, we had a concert. At that point, there were some ballplayers in Philadelphia who had come to Christ, including 76er Julius Erving, Mike Schmidt, Bob Boone, Garry Maddux of the Phillies, and Bobby Jones, whom we had just acquired. They all shared messages and then we brought out a top Christian singer."

Pat continued, "That first one was a huge success. So much so that we decided to have a second one in the spring. We did that for five years. So while I was there, we had ten of them—two each year. Well, that event has since been utilized by teams throughout the sports world at every level. These 'God and country' nights have prevailed everywhere, including here in Orlando where we have had one every year for thirty years with a Christian artist and a ballplayer speaking and sharing their faith."

Pat's vision to invite Jesus into the ballpark has been a tremendous success ever since that first night. Today, stadiums, arenas, and smaller venues across the globe have used the blueprints for the event while using names like Faith Night or Christian Night at the Ballpark. Pat, however, still prefers the original title, saying, "I like God, Family and Country Night. I think that kind of covers the whole waterfront." Pat also added, "Now, that spring, we did have a Jewish night. It didn't fill the building, and we didn't have a postgame concert, but that is how the whole thing started."

Pat's faith in Christ is known by all who know him. I spoke with a dozen people who referred to Pat as a religious person or talked about how he shares his faith without getting on a soapbox. Fellow Christians marvel at Pat's persistence to not only share Christ but to clearly live out a life that exemplifies his teachings. Pat's faith in Christ is not a priority in his life because he says it is; it is a priority because the rest of us can see it.

In professional sports, faith in Christ is not a top priority. Evangelizing to the people of that world required finesse. Instead of standing on a street corner outside the stadium sharing the gospel with everyone who walked by, Pat quietly help build a foundation and infrastructure that supports the sharing of the gospel in every city that hosts a professional sports team across the country, which equates to thousands of opportunities each year.

Pat has devoted part of his life to trying to change the culture of professional sports to include Christ. In many ways, he has succeeded. From his first luncheon with the FCA to the most recent All-Star Chapel Service, Pat is responsible for the name of Jesus being spoken front and center in arenas and buildings where teams and players often receive more honor. Not only was Pat able to use his career as a way to create successful methods to evangelize, but each method shared in this chapter was executed through Pat's actions instead of his words. ★

CHAPTER TWENTY-SIX

EVANGELIZE WHILE TALKING

Never Miss an Opportunity

Watching the ways in which Pat evangelizes without talking can be inspiring. The truth is, however, that many of us may not be in a position to start branches of national ministries in cities across the country. Instead, while on our journey to becoming advanced waymakers, we must find more common and relational ways to share the truth of Christ with others.

Upon being born again, Pat began calling everyone he knew to tell them of his experience. Many of his friends, family, and acquaintances were on the receiving end of those calls. One call went to a flight attendant from Eastern Airlines named Pam Smith. Pat said about meeting Smith, "I was going to the winter baseball meetings in 1967. We struck up a conversation and exchanged phone numbers."

A few months later, Pat met Jesus and called Pam in New York. "He was practically jumping through the phone," Pam said. I asked him, "What does that mean?" Pat continued to explain, and Pam finally said, "I want what you got. How do I get it?" Pat replied, "Come on down to Spartanburg, and I'll show you."

Once she was in town, Pat drove Pam to have a meeting with his pastor Alastair Walker. After the meeting, Pat picked her up, and she said, "Well, now I've got what you got!" Pat recalls, "It was overwhelming to see that happen. For me, as a new believer, to see someone changed like that was incredible. Pam has had a strong faith in the Lord ever since; that was fifty-four years ago."

More recently, Pat has used his personal relationships with others to either lead someone to Christ or encourage their walk. Barbara Albrecht, for example, has seen Pat's personal evangelism methods work up close. She said, "My husband, Bill, and I met him through his wife. I was involved in a Bible study with her. We were at a Christian women's club dinner, and Pat gave a message and invitation."

That night, Bill accepted Pat's invitation to accept the Lord. The two couples then began spending time together. Barbara said, "We went to some couples Bible studies. We went to several basketball games together. Pat was very influential and helpful in our Christian walk."

Howard Edington, the former pastor at First Presbyterian Church of Orlando, shared that Pat's ability to express his faith through words and behavior is the main reason key relationships he built were made to begin with. He said, "The initial conversation that led to the creation of the Orlando Magic took place on the pews of the church that I served in and where Jimmy Hewitt was a member."

Howard continued, "He has a faith that won't quit, and he is unashamed in his ability to share that faith and crystallize people to his way of thinking. He doesn't beat you over the head with it, but if you are in his presence, you are going to get a double-barreled expression of the Christian faith."

Howard was close to the DeVos family and preached at Rich DeVos's funeral. He said, "Ultimately, the DeVos family became the owners of the Magic, and their faith has also been unashamed and unapologetic. They embraced Pat Williams. Neither one of those men, Rich DeVos or Pat Williams, ever miss an opportunity to share their faith. I've seen it play out in so many different ways and in so many different places."

Do You Feel Unsettled?

Vince Nauss spoke about one of the unique ways Pat has used speech to evangelize and share his faith, saying, "I became a Christian in 1984. Pat was influential immediately by recommending a church for me to attend in the off-season. I remember Pat speaking and making an appeal for people to provide bicycles in China. You hear a lot of people saying, 'We need Bibles for people in this country,' but that wasn't Pat. He was after bicycles. He had vision."

Vince was the publicity director for the Phillies when he met Pat, but later became the president of Baseball Chapel, an organization Vince said was "solely focused on making disciples of young men in baseball." Before that, however, Pat offered him a role in the Orlando Magic office when they were building the team.

While he didn't end up accepting the job, Vince said Pat gave him the best piece of advice about whether or not to take the job: "Do you feel unsettled about where you are right now?" Vince replied, "No. I don't." Pat said, "Well, in my experience, when God is ready to move you, he will produce an unsettling in your soul." A year later, Vince resigned from the Phillies and started work with the chapel program because "he did feel unsettled." Pat's advice in this area of his life led Vince down the path God had for his life, and now Vince says, "I give out that same advice all the time now."

Mike Burch is another example of someone passing along godly wisdom learned from Pat. In 1991, a newly married Mike began a role as publicity coordinator with the Magic. His wife, Kelley, also filled in as Pat's assistant for about six months. They both were able to get to know Pat really well during that time and "see God's hand" on the timing of it all. Mike said, "My wife and her family led me to Christ while I was in college. Then coming to work for Pat, I was able to see what a godly leader he was."

Pat was able to share Christ with Mike through conversation and behavior. Mike, however, also found Pat's evangelism method somewhere else—in his books. Mike is one of many who have been influenced by Pat to read more. Mike says he now reads two hundred books a year, including many of Pat's titles. He says that he is able to see the influence of Christ in much of Pat's writings, saying, "Every one of his books goes back to God, no matter who he's writing about and no matter what the lessons are. He does such a good job of tying the fact together that all of this is nothing without the foundation of the Lord."

Now a father, Mike has taken his son to meet Pat and some other familiar faces around the NBA to not only introduce his son to some great leaders but also to introduce him to leaders who are "men and women who care about God." Like Pat has done for him and others, Mike is sharing the ultimate waymaking lessons of God and Christ with the next generation. ★

CHAPTER TWENTY-SEVEN

SPEAK UP

The Business of Helping People

For decades, Pat has been one of the most sought-after public speakers in the country. Pat is able to combine his Rolodex memory with a reservoir-deep knowledge of culture, history, jokes, quotes, and personal stories to craft speeches that leave a lasting impression.

Great waymakers are usually great communicators who use opportunity and influence to speak up. And in a world made up of great communicators, Pat Williams stands tall.

Jim Schnorf founded a company that booked professional sports speakers. That is how he met Pat. The two became close friends, and Jim has heard Pat speak many times. Jim said, "He's an unparalleled speaker. He's never overly wordy. I've heard hundreds of people speak, including politicians and leaders of large publicly traded companies. Pat's in the top few speakers I've seen anywhere. He's undeniably the best in sports."

While Jim described Pat as a "lifelong learner," he was surprised to find out that the speaker he believed was unparalleled decided to hire a speaking coach, saying, "I asked Pat what led him to believe he could hire someone to make him a better speaker. Pat said, 'I can always get better. I've already been given one tip I think is invaluable.'"

The founder of the Washington Speakers Bureau, Harry Rhoads, where Pat has been on the roster of speakers for years, said, "The purpose of the speaking business is to help people. In Pat Williams's case, it's a no brainer, because that is what he's all about." Harry went on to describe what makes Pat such a brilliant speaker: "Rather than get up there and talk about himself and the great life he's had, Pat does his homework. Pat's really good at finding out why people want him to speak in the first place."

Harry talked further about the impact of Pat's speaking, saying, "Now, it's one thing if you're an entertainer; you're just going to get up there and entertain people. But if you're Pat Williams, you're going to have some life lessons that you can share with an audience in a way that is impactful, and that's going to help these people when they go back home."

University of Pennsylvania professor John Eldred remembers inviting Pat to speak at a trade show function he orchestrated and the impact it left on a particular member of the audience. John said, "We were having our annual meeting in Hershey, Pennsylvania. We talked about the idea of parents being in the ultimate leadership role. Pat did such a good job with that topic."

John can still remember the facial reaction of a wowed woman in the audience, which consisted of CEOs of dental manufacturing companies and their spouses. "This lady was so struck by the idea that to be a parent is to be a leader" and "what a good job Pat did talking about that message." He described why Pat was so well suited to broach the subject of family leadership, saying, "He's an inspirational leader. Somebody who, mostly as a role model, manages to practice what he preaches."

Before Pat speaks, he asks a lot of questions about the group he is speaking to, including what the goals of the group are and what this group needs to learn. Asking good questions is another trait of the effective waymaker. He then examines his life experience to craft his remarks and then speaks to the crowd without notes. Over the years, the impact Pat has had on his audiences has been tangible. For this reason, Pat has taken very seriously his preparation and opportunities to speak with others.

That's a Good Question

Speaking isn't always best done through sharing your thoughts and ideas for others. Sometimes, the best way to speak up is to ask the right question at the right time. Great waymakers ask great questions; this instinct is part of their lifelong-learner makeup.

Mike Durney, the son of Pat's first boss in sports management, Bill Durney, has noticed this exceptional ability in Pat from early in his executive career. He said, "After ball games, I would love to sit in at my dad's office. My dad, Pat, my older brother Bill, and the field manager would sit around talking after ball games for anywhere from twenty minutes to three hours. And Pat would just ask questions. I remember that he was a great questioner."

Years later, Mike and Pat connected at a trade show during the MLB Winter Meetings where Mike was selling a device for cleaning sports equipment called Laundry Loops. As they walked around the trade show floor, Mike again noticed Pat's ability to ask great questions, saying, "It's like he was twenty-four years old again. He would ask these vendors, 'Why does the bat have this shape? What's the difference between this wood and that wood?'"

Mike continued, "There was a guy there who specialized in catcher's masks and had a display of the history of catcher's masks. Pat loved that. He pointed to the ones he used as a kid and in college with the Marlins. He would ask the guy the most insightful questions." Mike reasons that Pat "has an interest in people, and that is why he asks them great questions."

Mike described the influence Pat's behavior in this area had on his life, saying, "To me, that inspiration has crossed over into aspects of my life, mainly as a classroom teacher. I try to be a good questioner as a way to learn and also to teach."

College basketball broadcaster Dick Vitale is also a member of the Washington Speakers Bureau. Dick spoke about Pat while the country was in quarantine because of COVID-19: "Pat's a master communicator. In the time we are facing today, with the coronavirus, Pat Williams would be a good guy to be around because he would try to encourage and look for those things that are happening, maybe in a way that's going to solve the problem."

"Everything I believe in, [Pat] represents. It's contagious, having him around you. He lives today like it is going to be the best day of his life."

Pat's influence has been so visible to Dick that, alongside former NFL quarterback Jim Kelly, Pat was a 2020 recipient of the John Saunders Courage Award, which is handed out at Vitale's annual gala and highlights the inspiration cancer survivors have shown others in their battle. Dick talked about why Pat was given this award, saying, "Battling cancer is a serious situation, and the bottom line is Pat always has that spark in his eyes. Pat is just a great humanitarian. He has great energy and enthusiasm. He's optimistic. Everything I believe in, he represents. It's contagious, having him around you. He lives today like it is going to be the best day of his life."

Waymakers may have the ability to influence and direct others onto positive trails for their lives, but with that influence comes the reality of having to speak truths. The truth may set us free, but that doesn't make it easy to hear or share. In the area of professional sports, talent comes and goes on a daily basis. Not every player who makes it into professional sports has longevity. For every Shaquille O'Neal there is a Harold Miner.

Shaquille and Harold were both first-round draft picks in the 1992 NBA Draft. Shaquille played for nineteen seasons, won four championships, and was elected into the Hall of Fame. Harold, on the other hand, was drafted with high expectations but wasn't able to reach them. His professional basketball career was over after only four seasons.

Knowing the high-risk/high-reward world of professional sports, Pat has tried to steer players early in their careers to make wise decisions regardless of how long they stay in the league. Pat's financial planner and family friend, Janet Wills, was on the receiving end of many Pat's-recommendation phone calls from players and coaches seeking her wisdom and guidance in the area of managing their NBA salaries.

Janet said, "He would connect me with them. I think he probably gave them the best advice of their career, because a lot of them ended up in the CBA or left the NBA in their first or second year. Not everybody makes it, even though they are really good. Pat kind of had an eye for that. He kept them encouraged, and he knew how to direct them without overtly saying, 'You aren't going to make it.' Instead, Pat would say, 'What are you going to do next? How can you translate this into something else?'" Janet added that because of Pat, "I've had two or three guys who have had successful careers, but not in the NBA."

Addressing the Nation

Waymakers use their voice as a tool to help others. For Pat, it didn't matter if he was speaking from a stage in front of a room of people about leadership or talking one-on-one with a friend on the phone about cancer. The result is the same—he makes himself available to help. His memory, research, and wealth of experiences lend themselves to making him a well-sought-after speaker, but I imagine he would be doing those things even if no one was calling to book him. Pat makes himself ready to speak up in season and out of season.

Most recently, and perhaps most importantly, Pat was asked to speak on the subject of NBA superstar Kobe Bryant's tragic death in a helicopter crash. On the stage at *Fox and Friends*, host Brian Kilmeade again invited his friend Pat Williams to help speak up to those who were hurting. This time, however, instead of being live on a stage in front of a few hundred people, Pat was delivering a message to millions.

"There's so much sadness," Pat said, addressing the nation. "I do want to talk to the country today, if I may, about this horrible feeling we all have. God knows the minute everybody is going to come into this world. He also knows the exact minute we're going to depart from this world. He knows. And in this period from birth to death, the real issue is—what have we done about Jesus Christ. By inviting Him into our heart, we're assured of an eternal destination in heaven. People are thinking about their own mortality. I think that's what's happened here. God is in control. Jesus comes into our heart, and that's the difference maker."

In a moment where the world is looking for help processing the untimely death of a sports superstar, Pat presented the only name that can help us all—Jesus Christ. In previous chapters, we discussed how Pat used actions behind the scenes as well as the word of his testimony to evangelize. His verbal presentation of the gospel on *Fox and Friends* in January of 2020 was a mixture of both. The moment showed the richness of Pat's gifting as an evangelist.

He used his words to speak publicly about Christ in a way he never had before. Days earlier, when Pat was asked to come on the show, Pat said he spent time preparing behind the scenes, saying, "I kept praying: 'Lord, what am I meant to be saying here? What can I say to a grieving nation that would be appropriate, helpful, and hopeful?'" After he found the words, he shared them on the broadcast, because, he said, "That's what the Lord led me to do."

What Pat didn't prepare for was the response. He said, "I had no idea what was going to be the outpouring from that interview. From every nook and cranny, I have heard from so many different people—many I didn't know—who just seemed to be deeply moved by those comments. I'm thankful that the Lord gave them to me and the Holy Spirit gave me the opening."

The overwhelming response Pat received was significant, the largest number of responses Pat has ever received after an achievement in his life. Humble Pat seemed surprised by the excitement, saying, "It's been quite an experience to see how the Lord took those few brief words and has stirred people up so, including Franklin Graham, who put it out over his whole network. It's fascinating to see the outpouring of emails, messages, and phone calls."

Third-world missionary Larry McFadden is a member of First Baptist Orlando alongside Pat and talked about how their church reacted to the *Fox and Friends* interview. "Everybody was talking about that, really," Larry said. "Matter of fact, my pastor mentioned it on Sunday morning after that happened. He said, 'Did you see Pat's interview? What an incredible witness.'"

Pat has been chasing visions his whole life, many of them long accomplished. Prayer has always been a component of how Pat prepares his speeches, but he probably never envisioned praying for the right words to speak up for Christ in a time of national mourning. But as Pat said, "God is in control." He certainly is, and on that day the Lord chose a mighty waymaker to deliver a life-changing message. ★

CHAPTER TWENTY-EIGHT

BUILD COMMUNITY

I Pray Your Eyes Would Open

In construction terms, a cornerstone is the foundational stone whose placement precedes how all other stones or bricks will be set. The entire foundation of the structure's position relies entirely on the cornerstone. The Bible describes Jesus as the cornerstone of our faith (Eph. 2:20; Isa. 28:20; 1 Cor. 3:11). Jesus, who was a carpenter, knew the importance of how things are built and explained to others in multiple scriptures how they might build something themselves.

Most notable is Matthew 7 (NLT), where Jesus says, "Anyone who listens to my teaching and follows it is wise, like a person who builds a house on solid rock. Though the rain comes in torrents and the floodwaters rise and the winds beat against that house, it won't collapse because it is built on bedrock. But anyone who hears my teaching and doesn't obey it is foolish, like a person who builds a house on sand. When the rains and floods come and the winds beat against that house, it will collapse with a mighty crash."

When Christ entered Pat Williams's life, the foundation on which everything that happened after that was set against that cornerstone. Every intentional effort Pat made to stay humble. Every empathetic gesture made to a person near him. Every career success. Every adopted child. Every book written or marathon run. All this was built on solid rock because of Pat's relationship with Jesus Christ.

Pat has accomplished many great things and been a waymaker for so many individuals, but it is his work building up the communities around him that may be the greatest evidence of how Christ led Pat's life as a waymaker.

Dr. Des Cummings served as executive vice president of AdventHealth, whose faith-based organization is America's largest admitting hospital. Pat is on the board of this Orlando-based healthcare system. Though recently retired, Dr. Cummings has seen Pat's community-building work firsthand and shared another biblical example to describe Pat's effectiveness in that area.

"Pat is like the story of Elisha at the city of Dothan. What happens is the Syrian army king has basically been saying, 'I've got to capture Elisha, because he's tipping off the Israelites to every step I take when I tried to attack them. They successfully avoid me and move away, and I'm frustrated at each corner because I want to capture their territory.'"

Dr. Cummings continued, "So he sends his army to go and get Elisha. In the morning, the young man who is an apprentice of Elisha sees the Syrian army camp waiting. He yells to Elisha, 'What are we going to do?' Elisha stands beside him and instead of giving him a lecture on what God can do, he does the thing I think Pat does for all of us. Pat is capable of giving inspirational talks, but one-on-one he stands beside you like Elisha did with that young man and prays that your eyes would be open. I think that's the gift that Pat has, to help us imagine the path that God would have us walk by simply raising our eyes, raising our vision, raising our aspirations."

Dr. Cummings described Pat's role on AdventHealth's executive board as "dual purpose." First, it is "to develop the strategy for the hospital to achieve the healing ministry of Christ" and then "to help us find friends and donors who really believe in that and want to make it one of their core causes that they champion." Pat's involvement has helped AdventHealth grow to a healthcare system with thirty hospitals that not only impact the community of Orlando but cities throughout the country.

The leader of the AdventHealth Foundation, David Collis, elaborated on Pat's involvement with the hospital, saying, "When he had multiple myeloma, he wanted to raise money. So we went out into the community and were raising money with Pat to support the research and physicians who were in the multiple myeloma space. He's connected us with so many different people. The Solar Bears were a group that played hockey in the arena in the off-season. Pat connected us with the team owners, and they were very supportive of [AdventHealth for Children]."

David added that when he heard about the creation of the Pat Williams Leadership Library, he quickly called Pat to support the cause. He said, "I got to be the first donor. It was just a small way that I could give back for everything he's done for our community. For me, personally, when you lead a foundation that raises $20–$30 million a year, his leadership on that board helps us raise that money because people look at the hospital and who's involved with it."

The Skyline of Orlando

In addition to his work on the board of hospitals, Pat's community influence has stretched to Florida universities as well. Dr. Bill Sutton, who has worked as a professor at Florida colleges University of Central Florida (UCF) and University of South Florida (USF), described Pat's involvement in the recent approval and construction of a $60 million downtown UCF campus, saying, "He had a lot to do with the new building being built. Pat was the PR guy that was out in front. Pat was mobilizing the community. Pat was explaining why it was a good idea. Pat was building the bridges with different community organizations to get their support. I mean, he was an ambassador."

Dr. Sutton also shared how Pat influenced his career path, saying, "I was having regular contact with Pat while I worked at the NBA, and I said, 'I'm ready to go back to teaching,' and Pat goes, 'Do you know the DeVos family started a program at UCF? Why don't you come down here and join this one?'" Bill was convinced by Pat and others to come teach at UCF, and because of that, he added, "Pat's had quite an influence on me."

Another Florida professor and community leader who has been influenced by Pat is fellow UCF professor Dr. Richard Lapchick. Sutton and Lapchick worked closely together on various school and community projects and on occasion would have Pat address their students. During his address, Pat would tell students underneath Sutton and Lapchick that "I hope you understand that you are being coached by the equivalent of Michael Jordan and Scottie Pippen."

Dr. Lapchick, who first met Pat after he showed interest in learning more about Dr. Lapchick's previous organization's training on diversity and inclusion as well as gender violence prevention, talked about Pat's influence on the people of Orlando, saying Pat "encourages people to not only have more breadth of interests and understanding, but to be better citizens."

Pat's contribution toward the building up of any area within the Orlando community was first made possible because of his vision and call to bring pro basketball to central Florida. Many people have attributed the continued growth of the Orlando area to the persistence and determination Pat used to fight for the city of Orlando when hardly anyone else would've given the city a second look.

Former Orlando mayor Bill Frederick said, "Pat's presence in the ownership group gave credence to us having a real shot at getting a team in Orlando because we had somebody who knew what he was doing. Getting our first professional team here marked the transition from a small-town community to a major urban center."

Magic broadcaster Paul Kennedy noticed how Pat laid significant foundational blocks that helped shape the community of Orlando, saying, "Pat is the pied piper who brought the NBA to Florida. That's astonishing. To the small, little town of Orlando which basically had only a theme park at Disney. The skyline that exists today in Orlando is there because of Pat."

Before becoming a sportswriter for the Athletic, Josh Robbins covered the Magic for the *Orlando Sentinel* starting in 2009. While Josh doesn't have an eye-witness account of what happened with the building of the team, he spoke how the community at large views Pat and his efforts in Orlando.

Josh said, "If it hadn't been for Pat Williams, what had been a tiny little town of Orlando never would have had even a minuscule chance to land an NBA expansion team. Yet many people were involved. Many people deserve credit, but without Pat Williams there would be no Orlando Magic. If you were to have some sort of Mount Rushmore of Orlando's four most important people, there could be no doubt Pat would be one of them."

Everything Comes Back to Baseball

Pat, of course, is still dreaming of leaving behind something for the Orlando community to have and enjoy long after he goes home to be with Jesus—the Orlando Dreamers. Pat's first love has always been baseball. So many of his friends have wonderful stories of talking baseball on the phone with Pat. Moments before calling Pat the "pied piper of Orlando," fellow baseball fan Paul Kennedy shared that he had talked to Pat on the phone only a few days earlier when they "spent forty-five minutes talking about former Philadelphia A's manager Connie Mack."

Pat thinks and dreams of baseball. He always has. In fact, during one of our conversations about his incredible memory, Pat highlighted how he is able to remember so many details of his life in sports. He said, "I remember every teacher I had in high school and every teammate in college sports. I do. And the Phillies organization. I remember every player on the various teams that played for us."

Pat, of course, is still dreaming of leaving behind something for the Orlando community to have and enjoy long after he goes home to be with Jesus—the Orlando Dreamers.

How is Pat able to remember such an incredible amount of information and create his Rolodex memory? Pat answered, "Because sports is built around seasons that have numbers to them." Pat then went on to give a demonstration of what he meant after picking a random month and year of his life. "April of 1956," he said, for example. "Now I can go back and remember. I was about to turn sixteen. That was my sophomore year of high school. I was a catcher. Our pitcher was a left-hander named Howdy Cross. He went to Yale. Redhead. Great curveball."

While Pat will say many people in sports are able to recall their own sports history and have great memory recollection, even those who do will say that Pat is still in a class of his own because he seems to be able to remember names, numbers, batting averages, and statistics of every player he has ever seen or heard of.

Pat said his memory is so good because "that's all part of it, when you become a sports fanatic. Particularly baseball." Pat said he loves baseball above any other sport "because it's so individual. When you are up at the plate, you are not confused like at a football game where there are twenty-two people banging into each other and falling over one another. But in baseball, the great pitching efforts or the significant home runs stand out and stick to the wall.

"Plus, it's America's pastime," Pat added. "We all grew up with a father or an uncle or somebody who took us to our first game. And we still have memories of walking into the ballpark and seeing the beautiful green turf, the white lines down to the flagpole, sparkling scoreboard. We still remember the vendors coming around, hocking their dogs and their peanuts."

Pat helped build up the community of Orlando because of basketball, but for Pat everything always comes back to baseball. Over the years, Pat has passed on multiple opportunities to get back into baseball including an over-the-phone offer to become the general manager of the Baltimore Orioles. Pat said no to offers like that in order to stay in the basketball lane God directed him to travel after his salvation. Now in his eighties and retired from basketball, Pat finally has a green light from God to reunite with the game he loves, and once played, by embarking on a quest to bring Major League Baseball to Orlando.

Pat's focus on his favorite passion will still allow him to contribute to the continued growth of the Orlando area. If successful, Pat's efforts will likely create thousands of jobs, business opportunities, and long-lasting enjoyment for the citizens of the greater Orlando community.

Rick Vaughn is a new friend of Pat's. Rick was VP of communication with the Tampa Bay Rays for twenty years. Rick said about meeting Pat Williams for the first time, "He's eighty going on twenty-eight. His zest and inquisitiveness are not like a typical senior citizen. He's so impressive. I was a little skeptical on my way up there. I know the challenges of doing a baseball team down here, but I left the meeting excited about it. All because of his enthusiasm."

Good 'Ole Days

Regardless of how Pat's baseball adventure turns out, any community building he has done, whether it be his years in Chicago, Philadelphia, or Orlando, will be the result of God putting Pat into the world of basketball, a world where Pat has thrived as a waymaker.

Upon his retirement from the Magic, many parties were held and well-wishes given. At one event, they played a video for Pat where many people including NBA Hall of Famers, coaches, broadcasters, and executives all shared their thankfulness for Pat's career and his role in their personal lives. Their genuine comments speak to how Pat has not only been able to build up the communities but also the individuals within that community.

One of the first faces on the tribute video was Julius Erving, who played on the 1983 championship 76ers team. He pointed to a framed picture of that year's team and said, "These were the good ole days. You've been in the league over fifty years. I started my career in basketball forty-seven years ago, so we've had plenty of overlap. Our

Philadelphia experience was grand and successful. I think our Orlando experience was a great learning time for me—things that I've learned from you. The time I spent around you and your family has you way up there on my list of people who I love and admire and wish nothing but the best for. God has blessed you in a very special way, and you've blessed me in a very special way."

Former NBA commissioner David Stern left a message for Pat, saying, "You've been a part of the NBA for so long and an important part of each stop along the way, and it's finally time for me to forgive you for putting those Mickey Mouse ears on me when we granted you the expansion franchise. So you are officially forgiven. I love you."

The video ended with a tribute from current Magic CEO Alex Martins, which summed up how Pat has been so successful as both a community builder and a waymaker at the same time. He said, "I want to thank you for everything that you've done for us here at the Orlando Magic. If it weren't for you, none of us would be here. This entire organization would not have the great thirty-year history that we've had. It was your vision and your hard work that brought the Orlando Magic to central Florida back in the mid-'80s. I'm personally incredibly grateful for you taking a risk on a twenty-five-year-old to be your first public relations director in that first season in 1989. I'm incredibly grateful for the opportunity that you presented to me and the kick start that you gave to my career here at the Orlando Magic." ★

★ ★ ★

CHAPTER TWENTY-NINE

PRACTICE PROXIMITY

An Unanswered Question

At the beginning of this book, I posed the question, "Who do you want to be like when you grow up?" As we near the end of our time looking at the special qualities that made Pat Williams a waymaker, you have likely considered your answer. For me, however, a new question emerged during the course of writing this book—what have I learned most from my time with Pat?

Obviously, after writing a book of lessons on how to be like Pat, it would seem that I have learned a lot. I have. Yet during the course of my interviews with Pat's friends, family, acquaintances, and colleagues, I was asked this question a number of times. The same people who have known Pat for decades and whom I was leaning on to learn what it was about Pat that made him a waymaker asked me what I learned most from studying Pat's life.

I found this question to be both surprising and insightful. Many of the people I talked to are lifelong learners like Pat. They have conditioned themselves to ask good questions and seek insightful answers while listening to others.

When Pat activated his listening ability during his first meeting with Bill Veeck, he heard, "You can't control the win-and-loss column, but you can control everything else that goes on in your ballpark." That one sentence transformed the way Pat operated for the rest of his career. Pat credits that advice as being the foundation for his career success.

I want to share some of the final insights I learned about Pat that I have yet to share. These insights—which are the type you can only discover from looking someone in the eye or seeing them in person— were found in June of 2020 during a trip I took to Orlando to meet Pat in person for the first time. Even though I had spent a great deal of time on the phone with Pat over the years, I knew the impression that I had of him for this book wouldn't be complete or fully realized until we were able to meet in person. So I traveled from my home in St. Louis to Orlando to meet Pat.

An Authentic Experience

For the start of our long weekend together, Pat picked me up outside my hotel. Initially, he had asked me to stay with him at his home in Orlando; however, the same week I was to come he was also visited by some of his out-of-state children who then occupied the guest rooms. Thankfully, the appearance of his children at his home allowed me to see Pat in his role as a dad.

Around his children, I saw Pat open up in a way I hadn't seen during our conversations. Pat had been honest and transparent in the personal information he shared with me. Around his children, however, I noticed Pat allowed himself to not be the Pat Williams everyone knew from work or on the speaking circuit. Without that pressure, Pat told jokes that didn't land, but he laughed anyway. I noticed he would warmly smile every time his daughter Karyn or son Jimmy entered the room. He casually talked about fruit. Specifically, his love for Washington cherries—which would quickly disappear anytime Ruth brought home a bag from the store.

That weekend, Pat and I also made the two-hour drive to Sarasota, Florida, to watch his eight-year-old twin grandsons, Teddy and Jack, play baseball. At the game, I met Pat's son Bobby's family in person, including Bobby's wife, Mary Lynn. I watched Pat as he brought a book and two magazines inside the park to read. I felt like I was in a movie, because I had heard so many people tell me about Pat's constant reading habits at every free moment, and now I was experiencing that in person.

A similar feeling happened at other times during the weekend, including when Pat read pages of his latest book on World War II from his reading chair and when he read his five newspapers and tore out clippings to send to others. I later watched him hand a stuffed envelope of clippings to Bobby before we left their company.

I felt in awe as I took a tour of Pat's index card collection and rifled through hundreds of the most inspirational notes ever assembled and browsed his home library. Pat showed me his Franklin Covey planner, which housed handwritten numbers for thousands of the most notable names you could think of. The pages were brittle from decades of use. Pat also allowed me to flip through the pages of the study Bible he created, where every inch of space and margin had been filled with notes. Unreadable to the average eye. Pat read sections of them out loud to me, proving once again that Pat is not average.

The most notable of Pat-centric experiences happened during our first lunch together. Pat dropped me off at the door to get a table. I did. I then sat for a few minutes waiting for Pat to arrive, tape recorder on and ready for our first meal together. I was excited to partake in having a meal with Pat. So many people had told me stories about life-changing conversations and advice that happened during the course of a meal with Pat. Was I about to have one of those encounters?

Pat walked into the restaurant wearing an Orlando Magic mask. The waitress was standing at our table, and before he sat down, he said to her, "I'd like an omelet with tomatoes, peppers, and onions; grits; and an iced tea." Pat then looked to me to order. To quote a phrase Matt Lloyd said earlier in this book, "I was woefully unprepared." In the history of ordering at restaurants, I had never seen someone order in this manner. Even though Dwight Bain had warned me of this exact behavior, I still wasn't expecting it. "I'll have what he's having," I blurted out. Pat continued to order this way during subsequent meals. It became normal to witness. I learned to be prepared to order.

Back at the baseball game, Pat—or "Poppers," as the grandkids call him—was an active fan in the stands: "C'mon, Jack! Let her rip!" While Poppers is an incredible encourager from behind the fence, he also said he used to openly share more insightful comments but has since been warned by the grandkids to keep his constructive comments to postgame debriefings as opposed to yelling them from the stands.

Whenever there was a break in the action, Pat's head shifted down forty-five degrees toward his reading material of choice—this time a *People* magazine. "Did you know Kanye West and Kim Kardashian have a baby named Psalm?" Pat asked me without looking up. I was shocked to hear that sentence come out of his mouth. When I asked why he was reading that particular magazine, he offered that he likes to keep up with different types of stories. Again, the Pat I knew from the phone didn't read *People* magazine. The Pat I pictured from the phone only read war stories and presidential biographies. Pat even handed me the magazine when he was finished and asked me to play the picture search game in the back of the issue.

After his grandkids' high-scoring baseball game, I headed to dinner with Pat and Bobby's family. The two boys asked to be interviewed for the book. They shared, "We love playing catch in the backyard." They also wanted to talk about out how Poppers introduces them like an announcer whenever they pretended to be professional basketball players on the court behind his house. Without hesitation, Pat gave us and everyone else in the restaurant an unscripted demonstration of his backyard announcements: "Ladies and gentleman, stand and cheer. From the Chicago Bulls: Michael Jordan! Now, from the Orlando Magic: Shaquille O'Neal!"

> Pat's disarming behavior also revealed him to be exactly what so many others had described him as—authentic.

During our dinner conversation, I also learned that Pat has three honorary doctorates of humane letters from schools in Florida, Pennsylvania, and Indiana, respectively. Pat said, "Now the problem is that people with real doctorates are not too thrilled because they actually earned their doctorates and I just showed up and made a speech." He also quipped to me, "Now on the front of your book, you can call it *How to Be Like Dr. Pat!*"

My trip to Orlando included a lot of conversation. On that trip back and forth from Sarasota, I spent more than four hours alone in the car with Pat, listening to unheard stories and getting a history lesson in Orlando architecture and culture. Pat also spent time asking me deeper questions about my life than he had previously done. These types of interactions helped me understand more about Pat's uniqueness. Pat's disarming behavior also revealed him to be exactly what so many others had described him as—authentic.

I had my own authentic, yet unexpected, waymaker moment with Pat during this trip. It occurred when Pat brought up the subject of my health on our way to the airport to catch my flight out of town. I became overweight while I was battling a gambling addiction. While I had found deliverance from my sin issue through Christ, I had yet to lose the weight, which was the last remaining evidence of my old life. Pat used his physical education degree and years of professional sports experience to encourage me on some things I could do to start a weight loss journey. Pat asked, "Can you walk a mile?" "Sure," I responded. Pat said, "What about two? Three? Start there. I'll be your partner for accountability. You need to do this for yourself and your family."

This conversation wasn't how I envisioned the end of my weekend with Pat to go. For whatever reason, I never thought he would get so personal with me about self-improvement. I had limited how Pat could benefit or encourage my life to the inspiring quotes and stories I had been writing and talking to him about. Yet, a week later, my first call from Pat came: "Have you been walking?" he asked. "Yes," I responded. "I did three miles almost every day this week." "Good. Good," Pat said in that paused cadence I was so used to hearing. "Keep it up, and you'll get there."

My visit to Pat took place in June of 2020. When I talked to him the following January, I shared the good news. "Pat, I'm down nearly fifty pounds since I have seen you." "No!" he exclaimed. "How did you do it?" I kept it simple. "I did what you said. It made all the difference."

Having my own personal waymaker moment with Pat allowed me to recognize something special about him, which was that he was the same person that I had been talking to on the phone for several years. That fact would have been impossible to realize had I never met Pat in person. I would've always wondered if I was getting the real authentic version of Pat on the phone or a highlight reel of who he wanted to look like.

Initially, I had thought that Pat had begun to let his guard down during my stay there, but then I realized the truth—Pat's guard was always down. From our first interview to my weekend in Orlando years later and most recently as my weight loss waymaker, Pat has stayed true to who he is. I learned that to know Pat at all is to know the real Pat.

Live in the Silver Lining

In a world full of social media profiles, where we only highlight the best parts of our lives to others, I was expecting Pat to do the same thing. He couldn't, though. His life hasn't been lived on social media. He doesn't act, perform, or share his life in a way that hides things the world may view as less favorable or noteworthy. Instead, Pat lives a life of truth. His world has been in full view of everyone for years.

Newspapers in every city where he has managed have profiled Pat's life. *Sports Illustrated* has done articles on Pat and his children. For decades, television programs in the Orlando area have featured annual visits into Pat's home to see what he and the kids are up to. Pat may not have social media, but his life has been posted for decades. Pat, however, wasn't one way in front of the camera or on the court and then a different way when he was at home or in the locker room.

Pat's ability to be the same person to everyone in every situation comes from his ability to "live in the silver lining." At least that is what Brian White said about Pat's persona. Brian is married to Pat's daughter Karyn. Brian and Karyn are musicians living in Nashville, Tennessee. Karyn records Christian music and has recently joined Michael W. Smith on tour. Brian is a successful producer, performer, and songwriter, having written hits for Jason Aldean, Rascal Flatts, Danny Gokey, and others. They happened to be in Orlando during my visit, when I met them at a local coffee shop. A few unseen observations about Pat came forth at this meeting. Pat's ability to live in the silver lining was the most valuable.

Brian said, "When the storm cloud comes, Pat doesn't live in the cloud. He lives in the silver lining. Maybe that's a mindset he developed as a kid." Karyn added, "That was a defense mechanism he developed as a kid to find the good, stay busy, and stay in the silver lining."

Brian continued, "When all you ever wanted to do was play professional baseball and you get to the place where your team says 'Hey, we think you'd be better off in the front office,' at what point do you not go, 'I got to go home for a while and just think about this because I want to be a professional baseball player.' Maybe even get bitter. Pat said, 'Yeah, okay.'"

"He has almost a little-kid mentality where he sees everything as a new adventure," Karyn said. She also remarked that her father's desire to see good in all circumstances can sometimes "go a little too far at times." She said, "He saw cancer as an adventure. I told him, 'This is not an adventure! This is horrible!'" Soon after that talk with Pat, however, Karyn was able to witness how Pat's silver-lining living lifted up those around him.

She said, "I went to one of his cancer treatments one day, and he walked around and said hi to everyone by name. They were like, 'Hey, it's Mr. Williams,' and it's like this party erupted in the treatment center. I was expecting a funeral parlor, but he walks in and encourages them and gives out high fives. I guess you could say he finds the silver lining a heck of a lot quicker than the average person."

"It's a God thing," Brian said. "He has this supernatural, amazing relationship with the Lord where he sees living in the silver lining as his calling to take whatever the circumstance is and flip it."

Karyn shared another story about when she was working as a real estate agent in Nashville but was having trouble selling houses. "The market is weird. I don't know if I like doing this anymore," she told her father one day while they were together. Pat responded to her self-proclaimed pity party with a hug and the words, "I could argue that, for you, real estate is a ministry. When people are coming here and they need a home, that's going to be the home that they're going to raise their family in. Think about all the Lord's going to do in that home."

A hug, a note for how to live in the silver lining, and a piece of advice for how to see your life as God sees it is exactly what makes Pat such a remarkable waymaker.

A hug, a note for how to live in the silver lining, and a piece of advice for how to see your life as God sees it is exactly what makes Pat such a remarkable waymaker. Successful waymakers are pity-party bouncers. They remove you from the state of mind that says, "I can't," "Why me?" or "It's too hard." He has done this for his daughter when she was struggling to sell houses. He has done this for strangers trying to overcome cancer. He has stood in parking lots and done this with colleagues trying to navigate life after being fired. Pat empathizes, encourages, and then highlights a new path for someone to take or at least offers a new way to look at the path they are already on.

In the end, Pat sees each of us in a better position than we see ourselves. He knows God has a plan for each of us. Because of experience, he also knows that storm clouds pass, and testimonies arise out of the ground like rainbows when they do. Pat mixes his experiences with a portion of wisdom, friendship currency, and empathy to guide those who come to him. He's always ready to help someone and always interested in getting to know them so he can help them get further on their life path.

What I Captured

At the beginning of this chapter, I said I would share the most important lesson I learned from Pat. While every lesson I have learned from Pat provides immense value in its own way, there was one that stood out above everything else. Similar to how Pat learned something from Bill Veeck in their first meeting that guided his life from then on, I, too, learned my most valuable lessons from Pat within moments of meeting him.

In our first conversation, Pat told me, "I keep close to the things that are important to me." He followed that thought up by saying, "It's amazing what you can accomplish in sixteen hours a day, if you stay close to the things that are important to you. Don't do things that are really not leading you anywhere toward your goals in life. I think all of us are capable of accomplishing a lot more than we do."

In the years that have passed since he shared those words, I have thought about them almost every day. When I wake up, I consider what is important to me. My relationship with God. My family. My ministry. My writing. I then think about the tasks of the day and ask myself if those tasks will lead me further down the road toward my goals. I'm not always perfect in how I spend my sixteen hours, but Pat's lesson has given me a framework for each day. And isn't that the ultimate goal of a waymaker? To get someone to move forward each day on the path that God has for them?

You may find one of the other lessons from "Waymaking 101" or "Advanced Waymaking" to be better suited to get you down your particular paths. For me, however, I know that striving to be like Pat Williams in this area has gotten me further along in life and allowed me to live with purpose and passion. I hope that you, too, can begin to practice some of Pat's waymaker lessons. I believe they will help you find your way further down the path that God has created specifically for you. ★

john@testimonyhouse.org

We would love to hear from you. Please email your comments about this book to John Simmons at the above address.

For more information on the author or his ministry, please visit:

testimonyhouse.org

Other titles from John include *Finding Faith* and *God Has a Sentence for Your Life*.

CPSIA information can be obtained
at www.ICGtesting.com
Printed in the USA
JSHW081405170723
44897JS00003B/30

9 781642 258257